HOLD ONTO HOPE

HOLD ONTO HOPE

Finding Clarity Amidst Life's Challenges

Published by the Power Writers Publishing Group in 2025.

Copyright © 2025 Christine Ross

All Rights Reserved. No part of this book may be reproduced by any mechanical, photographic, or electronic processes, or in the form of a phonographic recording. Nor may be stored in a retrieval system, transmitted or otherwise be copied for public or private use other than for 'fair use' – as brief quotations embodied in articles and reviews, without prior written permission of the author.

ISBN: ISBN: 978-1-7635809-7-8 Print

ISBN: 978-1-7635809-8-5 eBook

A catalogue record for this book is available from the National Library of Australia

Design and layout by Andrew Davies
Project Management by Jane Turner

Disclaimer

Any opinions expressed in this work are exclusively those of the author and are not necessarily the views held or endorsed by others quoted throughout. All of the information, exercises and concepts contained within the publication are intended for general information only. The author does not take any responsibility for any choices that any individual or organization may make relating to this information in the business, personal, financial, familial or other areas of life. If any individual or organization does wish to implement the ideas discussed herein, it is recommended that they obtain their own independent advice

CONTENTS

INTRODUCTION	7
CHAPTER ONE: Any Ordinary Day – How Life Can Change in an Instant	13
CHAPTER TWO: Step 1 – Creative Visualisation – The Power of Our Imagination	35
CHAPTER THREE: Step 2 – Beliefs – Perception V Reality	47
CHAPTER FOUR: Step 3 – Attributes – Your Inherent Strengths	65
CHAPTER FIVE: Step 4 – Standards – Your Secret Weapon	77
CHAPTER SIX: Step 5 – Expectations – Whose Are They Anyway	83
CHAPTER SEVEN: Step 6 – Values – Your Inner Compass	107
CHAPTER EIGHT: Hope – Find the Glimmer in Life's Darkest Moments	117
CONCLUSION	121
ABOUT CHRIS ROSS	123

INTRODUCTION

What if I told you that one ordinary day could change everything? That a single moment unexpected, unplanned, could alter the course of your life forever?

This book begins on one of those days for me. A day that started like any other, but ended with a phone call that would turn my world upside down. It was the day my son Tom had a life-changing accident in a third world country, setting us on a path filled with fear, uncertainty, and pain. It was a journey I never could have prepared for, and yet, it was one that would ultimately reshape not just my life and my family's, but also how I viewed what truly mattered.

In these pages, I invite you to walk with me through the moments that broke me, and the steps that helped me rise. This isn't just my story, it's a universal story of what it means to face life's unexpected challenges and find a way to move forward with hope, courage and purpose.

Throughout this book, I share the powerful 6-step journey that emerged from the darkest days of my life. These steps are more than a path to recovery, they are a blueprint for rediscovering yourself, aligning with your values, and creating a life that feels authentic and fulfilling. They can guide you through moments of upheaval in your personal life, your career, your business, and your relationships, helping you turn challenges into opportunities for growth and transformation.

Whether you're navigating a crossroads, searching for clarity, or simply feeling stuck, this book offers tools, reflections, and, most of all – hope. It reminds you that even in life's most difficult moments, there's a way to unearth strength, purpose, and joy.

This isn't a story about tragedy, it's a story about resilience. It's about finding the extraordinary within the ordinary and choosing to live with intention, no matter what life throws your way.

I invite you to explore the many resources we've prepared to inspire and support you on this 6-step journey. By scanning the QR code below, you'll access an exclusive webpage designed just for our readers like you. There, you'll find a free downloadable journal to document your progress, and three meditations – including a guided conscious visualisation, a centering meditation for grounding and relaxation, and a mindset meditation to quiet that pesky inner chatter – and we all need that sometimes.

Each chapter also features thought-provoking Reflection pages to help you gain deeper clarity as you navigate each step of your journey.

If you're ready to take responsibility for your own life and commit to real change, the six steps in this book have the power to transform the way you think, feel, and live. These steps are designed to help you uncover what truly matters, and guide you toward a life filled with clarity, confidence, and purpose. Remember, some of the thought patterns holding you back have been with you for a long time. They won't disappear overnight. So, be kind to yourself as you work through this process. Practice the exercises in each step consistently until they become a part of your new go-to mindset. I promise, with patience and persistence, you'll begin to see your life turn around in ways you never thought possible.

So, as you turn the pages of this book, I hope you find pieces of your own story here. I hope you feel seen, supported, and inspired to take steps toward your own extraordinary life.

While life can be unpredictable at times, the way forward is always within your reach.

From my Heart to YOU.

Chris Ross

*I like the night.
Without the dark,
we'd never see the stars*

STEPHENIE MEYER

CHAPTER 1

ANY ORDINARY DAY
How Life Can Change in an Instant

It's summer, 2018. We're living on North Stradbroke Island managing a resort we'd taken over in 2013, transforming it from being rundown to sought-after through sheer hard work and our extensive background in business management. But despite the success, I was struggling emotionally. I couldn't understand why I felt so low all the time. People often commented about how lucky we were to live and work on one of Australia's most beautiful islands, yet I always felt lost and lonely. Outwardly, I pretended to cope, but inside I felt hollow. Numb. Nothing really mattered.

After Tom's accident in 2012, we'd decided to sell our dream home to purchase the management rights to the resort on Minjerribah, right or wrong! It was possibly a wrong decision looking back, as we weren't thinking clearly after the trauma we'd all just experienced. My marriage felt like a shadow of what it had been, and I missed my family terribly, and worried constantly that we weren't there for them when they needed us. Overall, it felt like our life was a complete clusterfuck. We had met some wonderful people on the island. Friends who remain close to this day, but nothing could fill the ache in my heart and the deep feeling of failure mixed with regret. A great combo!

This emptiness went on for what felt like years. The drinking to numb, the reading to escape, and the working long hours to avoid being with myself, all took their toll. One morning, I woke up feeling completely detached from the day ahead, dreading the act of having to pretend to care for all the guest's arriving that day. I stepped into the shower, and halfway through washing my hair I started crying. This was nothing unusual, however this time, I couldn't stop. Tears poured down my face, mingling with the water as my body heaved with sadness, and I collapsed to the shower floor. It was as if something inside me finally broke, and I could no longer hold it in. I had to face the fact that I wasn't coping. I was just masking my pain. Pain that needed to be released. I just didn't know how to begin that journey, and to be honest I was terrified of what I was holding within.

I'd always thought I had to be brave, had to be tough, people were depending on me. I couldn't let anyone see that I wasn't coping, that I was vulnerable, depleted. After all, I'd been through hell and back and survived, right? Here I was, a mother of two, a wife, a friend, a successful businesswoman, a big sister, and a mentor to young entrepreneurs. There was so much to prove. I couldn't let a little thing like my son Tom's accident break me!

So, why wasn't I coping?

My husband Pete, encouraged me to visit our local doctor, a beautiful woman who listened intently to what I was saying. She looked at me and said, "Chris, I think you are suffering from adrenal fatigue, and quite possibly PTSD with a range of related symptoms that I'd like to do some tests on. However, I honestly believe you haven't dealt with the pain and loss from your son's accident."

"Really," I replied. "I understand I'm fatigued, but I feel like I have dealt with Tom's accident."

"Really?" She raised an eyebrow. "How about this: I'd like to recommend some further tests, and maybe you could try talking to a good psychologist – it can't hurt, right?"

After that morning in the shower, something inside me shifted. It wasn't a sudden revelation, but an undeniable awareness that I couldn't keep going this way. Pretending wasn't an option anymore. I didn't know exactly what the way forward looked like, but I knew I had to find one.

In the months that followed, I was introduced to an incredible coach who would change my life. She encouraged me to open my heart, to let go of the pretense and really look at my life, at my routines, my relationships, and my own thoughts. I realised I'd lost sight of myself somewhere along the way, living on autopilot, going through the motions, ignoring the questions that had been simmering beneath the surface.

I started journalling, giving space to thoughts I hadn't dared explore in years. In those pages, I confronted some deep pain, guilt, and anger that I'd buried.

I started writing the story of the day my life changed forever. I didn't expect anyone to read it or even care. It was enough just to let it out. Piece by piece though, I began to unearth my values, the things that really mattered: hope, connection, courage, purpose, and love. They became my anchors, grounding me and giving me the courage to keep moving forward.

However, that story sat quietly in the background for years, until a chance meeting with my friend Maree who is a successful voice coach, changed everything. She invited me to read it to her, just so she could understand a chapter of my life she'd only heard of in bits and pieces.

When I finished reading the rough draft, I looked up to see my beautiful friend Maree sitting there, silent, tears streaming down her face. "I had no idea, Chris" she whispered. "This story is incredible. It needs to be told. You should share it.

This journey hasn't been easy. It's been a process of unlearning, of letting go, and of accepting that life wouldn't look the way I'd once imagined. But by letting go of those expectations, I began to rebuild myself from the inside out.

And that's why I'm sharing this story with you. Because maybe, just maybe, my story and the steps I took to heal myself can help you unearth what truly matters in your life too.

The Journey Begins

For me, the unravelling all began on January 23, 2012 – a date that is seared into my mind.

Our then, 20 year old son Tom, was celebrating having completed his 3rd year of Uni with his mates. Three young men feeling excited about life and looking forward to their first overseas adventure together, full of surfing, and snorkelling. The trip had been planned meticulously by Tom. He'd mapped out three fabulous weeks that included visiting different beaches, trekking into the high country and taking in the culture.

We had travelled to Bali as a family, and with other close friends a few times in the past, and we'd always enjoyed a fabulous, fun holiday. Tom was really looking forward to sharing the beauty of Bali with his mates.

One week into this adventure we got a call from Tom's girlfriend Maddie that changed our lives.

She rang to say that she'd just heard from one of the boys travelling with Tom, that he had had a fall and cut his head pretty badly, and he'd been taken by ambulance to a hospital, adding that he didn't have any other information at this stage. We thought this is so like Tom as we remembered all the times he'd come off his bike or skateboard growing up.

At the time, we were trying to finish off a renovation that had gone over budget and way over time, so we were a bit distracted and stressed out trying to keep the momentum up with the trades people involved in the renovation. We were keen to get to the point where our life could go back to some sort of normal before too long.

Even so, the phone call from Maddie really threw us, and it seemed like all we could do was wait to hear more, and I remember thinking something just didn't feel right!

By about mid-morning I couldn't put aside this nagging feeling in my heart that something was truly wrong – call it mother's intuition.

Back in Bali, they had taken Tom to the Bali International Hospital. 'Just another Australian who had come off a scooter' was the initial vibe we got from the medical team. But Tom hadn't come off a scooter.

The evening before, he and his friends had been at the local nightclub in Illuwatu, as young people are wont to do anywhere. Tom left the club before the others and wandered off down the stairs that led to the beach below. Somewhere on the steps he lost his footing and fell 6 meters off the side of the cliff onto a concrete rooftop, passing out where no one could find him.

Even to this day, Tom has little recollection of what happened, although he remembers waking in complete darkness to torrential rain and feeling a searing pain in his back. He remembers trying to move, and realising that he couldn't move his legs, then passing out again. He told me a few years later about how he'd left messages on his phone to us (his Mum and Dad), and to his girlfriend Maddie, thinking that they would be his last words of love because he was sure he was going to die on that rooftop. I can't begin to imagine what that must have felt like, being cold and alone in the dark. So much courage there.

As it was, he wasn't found until early in the morning when a young Balinese lifeguard heard Tom cooeeeing, and managed to get Tom off the roof with the help of quite a few of the other local men. They took him to the resort he was staying in, and rang his room to inform his friends that they had found Tom.

Tom's friend Ben rushed to reception to find Tom wrapped in a floor rug, white as a ghost, covered in leaves, and his eyes closed. Poor Ben thought his friend since childhood was dead! The shock of seeing your friend like that must have been immense. Then Tom opened his eyes and said, "Oh hey mate, sorry to mess things up." Such a bloke!

Back in Brisbane, we had no idea where they had taken Tom, and my gut feeling was that we needed to find him asap.

First of all, we rang the Australian Embassy in Bali, but there was no answer. Then we rang the Australian embassy in Canberra and discovered the Bali consulate was closed because it was a public holiday over there. Fortunately, the lady who picked up the phone gave us the numbers of the two hospitals that Tom could have been taken to. We rang the hospital in Denpasar first, but they advised us that there weren't any Australians admitted that morning.

Then we called the Bali International Hospital, and a wave of relief washed over me when an Australian nurse answered the phone and told us that they had Tom there.

We asked if we could speak to Tom. So the nurse took the phone to his lifelong friend Ben who was travelling with him. Ben filled us in on the results from all the tests the hospital had run. It seemed that Tom had an unstable spinal injury and couldn't feel his legs, as well as having a massive gash to his head, and more frightening still, Tom was lapsing in and out of consciousness, and the doctors were insisting on operating straight away.

Ben was overwhelmed, and trying to hold everyone off until he was able to speak to us.

My husband Peter then got on the phone and spoke to one of the doctors. Even though the doctor wasn't easy to understand, we were able to establish that the x-rays had revealed a fracture to the C2 and T12 discs in Tom's back. The only option the doctor offered was to take Tom in for surgery straight away. Peter's response to that, in no uncertain terms, was that he was not prepared to give permission for our son to be operated on until we had more information.

Things got a bit tense at that point, with the doctor reminding Peter that Tom was over the age of 18 and able to make up his own mind. After advising him that the conversation was being recorded, Peter reiterated the fact that we did not give permission for our son to be operated on, and that Tom was in no condition to make a serious decision like that for himself.

The doctor finally conceded to wait, and we proceeded to find out as much information about Tom's injury as we could, as quickly as possible.

Firstly, we called a dear friend who is a surgeon, and he told us that if the diagnosis was correct, then Tom should only be attended to by a specialist spinal doctor, and to get him back to Australia as soon as possible because time was of the essence.

We looked for Tom's travel insurance documents. We were so grateful that Tom listened to his aunt who insisted that he never leave the country without travel insurance.

Thank goodness Tom didn't follow his first instinct to not bother about getting a travel insurance policy, his thinking was, I'm 20, what could go wrong?

Then we called the Travel Insurance company.

They informed us that he hadn't ticked the box that would enable us to speak on his behalf – WTF!

Meanwhile, time was ticking away as the young man who answered the phone told us we needed Tom's consent. He explained that if we could get the phone to Tom so that he could grant his permission we'd be able to make decisions on his behalf.

We tried to call Ben on his mobile. That was no use – it had run out of charge!

Fortunately, the beautiful Australian nurse was still on duty when we called the hospital, and she took the phone straight up to Tom's room. Our concern ramped up when Ben told us that Tom was fading fast, and that the only reason he hadn't choked on his own vomit was because he was there at the time, and was able to turn him on his side and scoop the vomit out of his mouth. The problem was that they had his head in a brace so he couldn't move and the morphine they were giving him was making him violently ill.

By this stage, I'm starting to feel overwhelmed and desperate, but I know we have to hold it together to support these amazing young men through this ordeal as we work our way through the process of getting them home – and we WILL get them home.

We explained what was happening with the insurance company to Ben so that he would understand the situation, and would be ready to take their call. By this stage Ben and Tom had not eaten for 24 hours, and they were both shirtless and shoeless. It was just sheer determination that was holding them together.

The insurance company called the Bali International Hospital, and the Australian nurse took the phone to Ben. Then Ben held the phone to Tom's ear, and Tom said… "YES!! YES YES YES" – our lucky YES!

It seemed to take forever to hear back from the insurance company. We have no idea what is going on, and I am worried sick that Tom could pass away at any moment.

Finally, they called, and all is well, and they are now able to work directly with us and together we will get Tom home. It will mean arranging an international emergency medical evacuation from a third world country for a young man with an unstable spine and head injury. This is not an easy feat by any measure, let alone making it happen within 6 hours. Yet we feel confident that we have a fighting chance with the insurance company and all of their resources, and we find the courage to keep going.

I finally look around my home and see that a small group of my family and close friends have gathered to support us. I had no idea how they knew what had happened, but I felt a deep sense of gratitude and love.

By this time it was around 5 or 6 pm. It had been a very long day. I slipped away and walked into our bedroom where I burst into tears. I screamed into my pillow. I cannot believe this is happening to us, to Tom. I am trying to come to terms with the dawning realisation that life may have changed irrevocably for our beautiful young man.

Throughout the night I stayed up and talked with the medical team in the emergency room in Australia. They were great and kept me up to date in terms of when the Medivac team was leaving Australia, and again when they arrived in Bali. Most importantly of all, they shared their assessment of Tom's condition on arrival. That included the fact that Tom's vitals were ok. They certainly weren't great, but notwithstanding the fact that his state was not as stable as they would have liked, at least his vitals were good enough for them to expect him to survive the flight back to Australia. Needless to say, I didn't sleep a wink that evening.

The first plan was to fly to Brisbane via Darwin, but during the night Tom's condition worsened and Perth became the destination of choice because it was the fastest route to get him to a major hospital in Australia. That mattered because the Medivac team doubted that he could survive the longer journey that would bring him home to us in Brisbane.

At incredibly short notice, we were booked on the next flight out of Brisbane that was going to Perth. We needed to be at the airport as quickly as possible, but I found myself kind of moving in slow motion pondering the question of what I needed to pack for the uncertain conditions that we'd found ourselves in. Basically, the only certainty we had was uncertainty, and the fact that Tom's well-being was the only thing that mattered.

Within 24 short hours the world had closed in on us, and our life pivoted 180 degrees on what was previously the most ordinary of ordinary days.

Back in Bali, Tom and Ben were finally joined by Phil who was the other friend Tom was visiting Bali with. Phil had stayed back at the resort to be the contact point for family members, and to arrange for all of their belongings to be packed up. I can't imagine how it must have felt for these young men who loved each other as if they were brothers, to see Tom teetering on the brink of death.

Apparently, none of them had eaten, and Ben and Phil were hunkered down beside Tom's bed on the cold tiled floor of the hospital to protect and support their mate. They told me that they felt grateful and much more confident of a good outcome once the situation was being overseen by the Australian medical team. But they knew they weren't out of the woods yet.

We left Brisbane in the early hours of the morning texting family and friends to let them know what had happened. On the flight over to Perth I had a kind of out-of-body experience. It's as if my conscious mind just couldn't cope with the situation. There was a desperate little voice in my head saying *this can't be happening to us! This only happens to other people.* Then I realised that we were those other people. Just ordinary people doing whatever it takes to get our son home.

We arrived in Perth in a daze five hours after boarding the plane. We followed everyone else to the baggage pick up area, and realised we didn't even know where we were going until I saw a man with a sign that had my name on it. I remember just feeling incredibly grateful that the insurance company had stepped up to the plate and taken care of everything, including our transport to Perth and accommodation for as long as we needed it.

One of the Lucky Ones

After dropping off our bags we walked down to the hospital. It was a 30 minute walk through the heart of the city on a 41 degree day. We found the emergency department, and asked if a Medivac had arrived from Bali. It hadn't. We were asked to wait in the waiting room. It was like being in a twilight zone with the bright lights and the sound of the ambulances coming and going for what seemed like hours. When the ambulance finally arrived with Tom in it, we saw that he was heavily bandaged. We moved over to be by his side, and the first thing he said when we walk up to him is "I'm sorry Mum." My heart melts and I have to turn away as great big tears begin to stream down my face.

It took another six hours for the medical team to stabilise Tom. During that time, he asked us if he would ever be able to walk again. My heart was breaking for my beautiful, athletic, full of life son. I don't know, I think to myself, as I take stock of the fact that we were with our son in the trauma ward of a hospital over 3,000 km away from our home in Brisbane.

Eventually, we met the head doctor who told us that Tom had a T12 incomplete spinal injury, and possibly a brain injury as well. We have no idea what an 'incomplete' or 'complete spinal injury' means, or what the 'T', 'C' or 'D' meant for that matter. It was then that they told us that he was a paraplegic.

At that point we were struggling to understand how that could be. Maybe we were unconsciously resisting taking the information the doctor was sharing with us onboard. I honestly don't know what was going on except to say that it was way too much for either of us to take in so late in the evening. I guess we were in shock as well. What was clear was that we had to dig bloody deep to find the courage to keep going.

Tom made it known that he didn't want to be alone that first night in the hospital, and he asked his dad to stay with him. And of course, Peter stayed with his son and his best mate. I walked back to the hotel, down the Murray Street Mall which took me directly to our new HOME, for who knew how long at that stage.

As soon as I got inside the hotel room, I slid down the door, fell to my knees, and collapsed to the floor, still holding all of Tom's clothes from Bali. I started crying and shaking uncontrollably as I came to terms with the enormity of Tom's injuries. Slowly a deep, cold sadness began to wrap itself around my heart as I crawled into bed and fell into an exhausted, disturbed sleep still clutching Tom's clothes and smelling his scent.

We were beyond exhausted, and numb from the shock of the previous 48 hours, digging deep to find the courage we needed to keep moving forward.

The next few weeks were madness, full of medical tests, major infections, the need for isolation, head injury trauma, high temperatures, you name it – Tom had to endure it. It was just one thing after another as Tom's body started to close down from the trauma he'd experienced and the drugs he'd been given. He couldn't be left alone for even one minute at that stage. One of us was always there with him.

If it wasn't for my beautiful Perth-based friend Helen, delivering home cooked meals and a gorgeous bottle of red wine most nights, I don't know how we would have fared each evening. We were just so drained and exhausted by the end of each day.

I'll never forget the afternoon when they told us Tom was well enough to have his head injury operated on. Among other things, he now carries the legacy of having 42 stitches in his forehead. We joke about Harry Potter having nothing on Tom.

It wasn't a laughing matter though, but at that stage (even though we'd received medical advice to the contrary) we were all hopeful that Tom would have a full recovery. In our minds, what that meant was that he would definitely walk again. We'd all heard stories of people who'd made full recoveries after serious accidents like Tom had, and we believed that Tom was going to be another one of those cases.

Weeks crawled by until Tom was strong enough to undergo the intense operation he needed to have on his spine. We came up with the idea of Red Undie Day to acknowledge the fact that Tom was a Super Hero. So many of the nurses and support team joined in. We even set up a Facebook page called Tom's Recovery Page, so that the multitude of friends and family who were always there for him could be kept up to date with the developments in relation to Tom's recovery.

Finally, the day arrived and it was over five hours before we finally hear that Tom is out of surgery. Pete spends the night of the operation with Tom. The next day we meet with the team of doctors to get their verdict on the outcome of the operation. When the head doctor delivered the news we didn't want to hear, he was pretty blunt. The long and the short of it was that Tom would never walk again. To put that into perspective for us, the doctor went on to say that he was one of the lucky ones because it could have been so much worse. Pete and I were shocked into silence by the news we'd just received.

How Tom managed to stay positive after that ruinous blow I could not fathom. Our brave courageous young man just held my hand.

The words *What the hell… how can Tom be a lucky one?* resonated in my head. The future, as I thought it would be for our family, was shattered into a million pieces at that very moment. I felt like I was being sucked into a crack opening up under my feet. I was spiralling down. The only thing I felt was that I needed to leave. I needed to be alone, to breathe, to think or NOT think – I really didn't know.

So I slipped away, not wanting Tom to see me with tears streaming down my face, struggling to breathe. Not caring about anyone or anything, I made my way down the hall, and past the waiting room full of hopeful parents, and families with children.

In a daze, I made my way to St Mary's Church on the hospital grounds which had been my sanctuary over the previous few weeks. I walked inside, and an instant feeling of calm and peace replaced the anxiety and desperation I was feeling only moments before. I found myself a quiet pew at the back of the church where I laid down and silently cried my heart out.

I was physically and emotionally exhausted, the likes of which I'd never felt before. Finally, I gave in, I let go, and I went to sleep. It was a deep and peaceful sleep that lasted for about two or three hours. I don't think I'll ever forget that beautiful period of respite where I found a sense of peace.

What followed was the establishment of a routine around Tom's care, including regular appointments with his physiotherapist and other specialists. Unfortunately, Tom developed multiple complications from all of the drugs he was taking, including fluid on the lungs and a rare bladder/bowel infection called *C. Diff*. This resulted in his room being locked down again, and our having to wear PPE to go anywhere near him.

Meanwhile, Tom kept running high temperatures and having to take drugs that made him hallucinate, not to mention having to endure endless tests. The toll this took on his body was heart breaking to watch. Among other things, his weight dropped from 70kg to 55kg within the first two weeks of arriving back in Australia. He was just skin and bones.

The day came when Peter had to return to Brisbane, as did Erin (Tom's sister) who was starting her first year at the Conservatorium of Music. Meanwhile Tom's friends arrived from Brisbane as did some of mine. People come and go, and we were constantly amazed at the lengths our family, friends, and people we don't even know, will go to help us. We were certainly loved and cared for.

Time to Move

About four weeks later we were told that Tom was going to be moved to a rehabilitation hospital in Shenton. It was the best, we were told, in the state. We were excited.

Eventually, the time came when all of our family and friends who had flown over to Perth to support us had to go back to Brisbane for work or other commitments. From that point on it was only Tom and me. We both felt really sad to say goodbye to everyone, especially Tom's girlfriend Maddie who has stuck with him through thick and thin right up to this day as I'm tapping the keyboard on my computer writing this book. Tears still sting my eyes when I think about Maddie's loyalty. She is Tom's rock, and she has never wavered in her love and determination to support him through whatever situation arises. Her love for Tom was not challenged, not even in the face of the life changing incident that turned up and rocked our world.

We cried together that night, and Tom and I made a pact to do whatever it took to get back to Brisbane as soon as possible. We were determined, however it turned out to be quite a challenge.

The day they moved Tom to the Rehabilitation Centre in a suburb called Shenton, which is near Subiaco in Perth, was a major event for us, and for the hospital. There were so many moving parts needed to bring everything together. Ambulances, nurses, and physiotherapists, and checking and double checking that all the medical records were transferred together.

At the same time, I needed to find accommodation closer to Shenton as our city accommodation was now too far away. The insurance company put me in touch with a lady who helps people find accommodation. We found a great little town house in Subiaco that was about a 20 minute walk or 5 minute car drive away from Shenton Park where Tom was staying. The insurance people handle the entire arrangement for me. It was perfect, and I felt a sense of home for the first time with my own kitchen and a little outdoor area.

At first, Shenton felt like a complete disappointment. We were shocked at how run down the place looked. Men were crammed into rooms with four and five others who all have high needs. We felt overwhelmed and concerned. Tom looked completely dejected. Thankfully he had some of his best friends from Brisbane visiting at the time. He didn't want any of us to leave, but they wouldn't allow anyone to stay overnight, so we all had to leave him in the evening after visiting hours. I felt so very sad and wondered what lay ahead for us in that new alien environment.

We discover that Shenton Park is an extraordinary rehabilitation centre for all sorts of rehab for many different injuries. The spinal section was filled with lots of men of all ages. It was starting to become apparent to me that this is very much a young man's injury. There were so many cases, all with their own story. And wheelchairs everywhere. There were wheelchairs on the lawn, in hallways, in the distance, in the car park, in the bathrooms, in the visitor centre. It was such a wake-up call. I was terrified and overwhelmed. I remember thinking – *We don't belong here*. It was just so confronting, so far from the everyday of most people's lives, including ours.

Nearly three months went by as our days were filled with learning what Tom had to do to carry out basic things like going to the bathroom, transferring himself from the bed to the wheelchair, and to do what used to be simple things like rolling over and sitting up by himself. He also had to learn how to wheel himself around, and more generally, learning about what a spinal cord injury like the one he'd sustained meant in terms of the way the rest of his life was going to look.

After a while, we started to find our way around and get acquainted with a few of the other people on the ward. There was 78 year old Jack, who had kicked his toe on the corner of his bed in the middle of the night and fallen forward onto his bedside table. This simple accident resulted in a broken neck. There was Michael, a soldier who was in Afghanistan and was shot in the back. He is now a quadriplegic and was in the hospital being treated for a case of debilitating bed sores, which we discovered can be a common part of a spinal cord injury if you are not careful. His mode of transport was to lay face down on a trolley bed and push himself around. Incredible really!

There was a room just off Tom's where a group of people gathered every day to sing hymns and pray around a man. I later spoke to his wife, and she told me he was in the surf with a friend, and coming back out he was hit from behind by a wave that caused him to fall forward into the sand and break his neck. He was only able to blink his eyes. Such a simple incident, yet so life changing and devastating. I was shaken to my core as I began to realise that YES – believe it or not, Tom is one of the lucky ones!

One day as we returned from a physio session, we found that a Spinal Cord Manual had been placed on Tom's bed. I couldn't bring myself to look at it, but Tom couldn't resist going straight to the section marked SEX. So much to learn we laughed, and he had plenty of time to learn it because he faced long weeks ahead.

There were lots of rehab sessions, challenges with learning to do everyday things like going to the toilet, dealing with numerous infections, and low moods. Tom wouldn't eat the hospital food, not that anyone was blaming him, it was pretty bland, so I made dinner for him every day. I'd walk there and back most days, and for a little while I had the use of a car which was heaven. We were a team Tom and I, and sometimes we weren't as this accident had challenged Tom to his core. This once independent energetic young man was now completely changed. However, Tom never once wished this on anyone else, he even said to me one day, "Mum I'm glad this happened to me and not one of the other boys, because I don't think they would have coped as well". I just stared at him. Really Tom! You are amazing.

I didn't wish this experience on anyone either, however, I secretly wished it wasn't happening to us. Whether we liked it or not, this 'is what it is' and we had to make the best of it. Otherwise, we would be going to a very dark place indeed. Both of us had touched its outer rim and decided that's as close as we wanted to get.

One day after a particularly challenging physio session we had a meeting with the doctors to determine Tom's ability to travel back to Brisbane. They told us that a bed had become available in the Princess Alexandra Hospital in Brisbane, and that I could escort Tom home. I was not so sure about that! I speed dialled the insurance team and they said they could organise to get Tom on a midnight flight that coming Friday, and perhaps send Pete over to support us. No, no, no, I thought, no way in hell was I going to take a fragile son in a wheelchair, with no professional support, on a plane trip back to Brisbane – that was not an option. I started to feel frantic. I called my girlfriend who's a nurse and talked to her. Helen suggested that we organise a meeting with the head nurse of Tom's unit first thing in the morning. I didn't sleep at all that night I was so anxious.

The next morning both Helen and I arrived at the same time. We waited until the Charge Nurse was available and then explained what the doctors had told us the day before. She was astounded and immediately assured me that that was NOT going to happen. She explained that this was a medically assisted transfer, not a discharge, but a hospital to hospital transfer, and that we would not be leaving there without a nurse escort. "The doctors are mistaken" she said. We like her, a lot! She has taken control calmly and professionally. We begin to breathe easy.

As I'm writing these words my heart is filling with pride when I'm reminded of the way Tom threw himself into the tough rehabilitation process, and doing whatever he needed to do to become well and strong enough to return home. Despite the pain and uncertainty around his future, my beautiful boy just never stopped trying his best, I remember getting a sense that if anyone had the capacity to live life to the fullest no matter what life threw at them, it was Tom.

I'll never forget how good it felt to hear that a spot had opened up for Tom to continue his rehab in Brisbane. A medical transfer was arranged with the support of the insurance company, and we were able to make the journey back to Brisbane accompanied by a nurse who had such an air of professionalism and calm about him that it gave us both the courage to take this next step in the journey of getting ourselves back home.

Finally, the pilot announced our descent into Brisbane, and we were met at the airport by family and friends with Maddie at the front.

Home after three months, home – not the same as when any of us left, but we are home.

After a quick hello and hugs all round, Tom was whisked off in the waiting ambulance to be taken to the Princess Alexandra Hospital and their Spinal Injury ward. This hospital truly is one of the best places for a spinal cord injured person to be.

Another two months went by as Tom was recuperating in the ward and becoming accustomed to his new life, and once again we meet so many families affected by this devastating injury. So many families whose lives were changed completely.

In many ways our Journey had just begun – but we were HOME.

Twelve years on as I am writing this book, Tom is now married to his sweetheart Maddie. Needless to say, it was one of the most emotional and inspiring weddings I have ever been to. We were surrounded by family and friends who supported us, and never left our side even when we were not at our best. Tom and Maddie now run an award-winning dog training school on the Gold Coast, and they brought our gorgeous granddaughter Bethany

Christine into our life in 2023.

And although life can be a struggle for Tom with endless pain and infections springing up from time to time, not to mention the careless ignorance of others, he rarely complains. Sometimes he'll say something like "I'd just like the day off today to be normal, and I promise I'll be back to my new normal tomorrow."

Any ordinary day can change the course of our lives in unimaginable ways.

When I reflect on my own journey – on those days of overwhelming uncertainty after my son's accident, it's sometimes hard to believe that hope and purpose could have come from such a dark time. When our lives take a complete left turn and we seem utterly unable to find our way back; when we slip into autopilot and pretend that everything is ok; when the truth is that nothing seems to matter to us anymore, it's in those moments that hope becomes our lifeline. Sometimes it's only when we're tested to our core that we realise the depths of our own resilience and strength.

It's often in these deep moments of challenge when we find ourselves in a mess on the floor or lost in the darkness, that we can uncover a spark of brilliance within us. What if we are not breaking down but breaking open? We don't always see our own strength and courage until life demands it from us. However, it's there, it's inherent, meaning that it's already within you. I've heard it said that we are born with a unique set of attributes designed to support us on our journey of life. I love that!

It's often the decisions we make on those ordinary days that are so powerful that they can change everything. Those simple yet courageous decisions to keep going; to get up each morning; to brush our teeth; comb our hair; and get out the door; to try to hope again.

Hope is not always about having all the answers. Often, it's simply about believing that something better lies ahead, and being willing to take those first small steps toward it. For me, hope was what kept me moving forward even when the path was unclear, and even when I wasn't sure if I had the strength or courage I needed to turn up every day.

And I want to share with you that hope isn't reserved for 'extraordinary' people. It's within all of us, waiting to be uncovered on any ordinary day. By choosing to take courageous steps forward, one by one, hope grows. It's a choice we make, and the intention to see beyond today's pain or confusion to a brighter, more fulfilling life.

There's power in stepping out of our comfort zones. It's often when we are feeling least prepared that we find our true selves. It's here that we uncover our inherent attributes – the strengths that are already within us. In these choices to keep moving forward, to dream, to make even one small change, we find our clarity and a deeper connection to what really matters to us.

You know, there's a quiet strength in taking ownership of your life, in choosing to shape it by design and not by default. Each step forward reveals more of who you are and what you're capable of. That's the essence of my 6-step program called ***BecomingYOU*** that is reflected in this book. I developed this program after finding my own way out of the dark hole I was in to help others rediscover and redefine what truly matters again, so that they can live intentionally, and make courageous decisions that align with their authentic self.

As I get close to concluding this chapter, I want you to think about your own journey. Are there parts of yourself – your own brilliance, waiting to be uncovered? Can you look back on those dark days and see your own inherent brilliance? Are there dreams that could be rekindled with even a small spark of hope?

By sharing my story with you in this chapter, I'm wanting to remind you that life's left turns can lead us to the deepest discoveries. And that by embracing each step forward, holding onto hope, and stepping into our courage, we can create lives of fulfilment, resilience, and purpose. I say that because you too, have a brilliance and a resilience within you that is waiting to be uncovered. And it all begins on any ordinary day.

Over the next few chapters, I'll guide you through the six transformative steps that not only changed my life, but have also helped countless men and women who've joined this movement to rediscover themselves after a life-altering event. These simple yet profoundly powerful steps are your gateway to reclaiming joy, clarity, and purpose, so that you, too, can embrace life to its fullest once more.

Simply scan the QR code below to unlock a safe webpage on my website that is filled with special gifts I've created to enrich and support the journey you're about to embark on.

The Journey Begins – Imagination is everything. It is the preview of life's coming attractions. Visualise your dreams to manifest reality and create your future.

Albert Einstein

STEP 1

CHAPTER 2

CREATIVE VISUALISATION
The Power of Our Imagination

In the words of Stephen Covey – "Begin with the end in mind." Covey's timeless wisdom invites us to envisage our destination before we take the first step. This means that we must create a vivid picture of what we deeply desire – not as a distant dream, but as a clear, tangible reality. Conscious visualisation is not about wishful thinking. It's about aligning our thoughts, emotions, and actions with the life we truly want to live. By anchoring our focus on the end goal, we ignite a powerful sense of purpose and direction, enabling us to navigate life's twists and turns with clarity and confidence. This chapter will guide you to harness the transformative power of visualisation, helping you craft a vision so compelling that it pulls you forward, even when the road gets tough.

So many people tell us that hope is not a strategy. And yes, in one respect they are right.

You don't want to be hoping for enough money to retire on and do nothing about it.

You don't want to be hoping for a healthy life and not exercise or eat well.

You can't expect a good outcome from an idea you've had if you never take that courageous step forward.

So no, hope is not a strategy.

However, hope is a strategy when you are experiencing a very challenging time in your life when you are feeling lost or overwhelmed, or sad, or grieving, or having to deal with changes in your circumstances that were unforeseen.

All of these emotions are real and need to be recognised for what they are – a loss of hope.

After Tom's accident, I went into a very dark time for many years. My life had taken a complete left turn and I had no idea how to find my way forward.

I went into autopilot, looking good on the outside but feeling completely lost and hollow on the inside. Nothing really mattered to me anymore. Yes, of course I loved my family and would do it all over again for any one of them, but I had become scared of the future. I just couldn't allow myself to dream that life would be safe again. I felt that if something so catastrophic could happen on a seemingly harmless holiday, on any ordinary day, then how could I find the courage to believe in tomorrow again. It felt as though the ground beneath me had been pulled away leaving me adrift in a sea of uncertainty and fear.

So imagine being told that learning to dream again was the beginning of healing. For me it was very confronting. I am sure there are many of you reading this book that have felt (or actually feel) the same way.

Then believe me when I tell you that I see you, and I hear you. Life's hurdles can make us wonder what's the use. But there is a use. These hurdles are a vital reminder that life is a journey, each phase bringing its own mix of joys, sorrows, and trials. Remember this, and you'll find the glimmer of hope amidst the darkness whenever adversity strikes.

Nowadays, I understand the value of dreaming and embracing the future. That's why I stress the importance of regaining trust in yourself, and unleashing your imagination to envision what lies ahead. Once we rekindle the ability to dream and paint a vivid picture of the life we desire, we can muster the courage to take those initial steps toward the next chapter, authored by none other than you.

That's not to say the unexpected will never happen – that's not what I'm saying here. However, knowing your Why will help you get back on your feet quicker the next time.

Creative visualisation is perhaps one of the best-known techniques for manifesting your dreams. Unfortunately, it is also the most misunderstood. It is the art of using mental imagery to produce a positive change in our lives. It has been successfully used in the areas of health, business, creative arts, and sport. It can have an impact on every area of your life.

There is nothing new, strange, or woo-woo about creative visualisation. You are already using it every day, in every minute of your life. It is the natural power of your imagination which you use constantly whether you realise it or not. Usually, our negative beliefs automatically kick in, and we unconsciously expect our lot in life to be full of lack, limitations, difficulties, and challenges. And to one degree or another, that is what we create for ourselves. Does that make sense?

So this chapter is about using your beautiful natural power of imagination to begin to create a life that you truly desire, such as one full of love, fulfilment, enjoyment, satisfying relationships, successful businesses, and whatever your heart desires for you.

In reality, most of us use our power of creative visualisation in a relatively unconscious way.

Russian athletes first used this technique to train for the Olympic Games in the 80s. They would spend 25% of their time on physical training, and 75% of their time mentally training by envisioning a great outcome. Needless to say, they outperformed many athletes at the following Olympic Games. These days, most of the best athletes employ creative visualisation as a central part of their training program.

Tom and his dad once heard Jonathan Thurston, who is a famous NRL football player, speaking at an event where he talked about how he used conscious visualisation to imagine himself kicking the ball between the posts and scoring every time he set up for a goal. How powerful is that!

So why not you?

That was what my coach said to me when we began this journey from self-doubt, confusion, and hopelessness, to finding a way forward again.

I'll be honest, it wasn't easy to begin with. I just had so much negative energy stored up that I didn't trust myself to ever believe life could be wonderful again.

Well, I'm here to tell you that creative visualisation is now the first step I take with my clients when we work through their limiting beliefs. I gently guide them into their heart space, unlocking their deepest desires and unearthing their true potential once more.

You see, when we allow ourselves to dream it, it will become a self-fulfilling prophecy.

How many times have you seen this work in reverse? Whatever one believes about themselves or their circumstances impacts their behaviour, which then impacts the results they get – often causing the initial belief to become true. For example, if you believe you will flunk a test, your study habits are likely to be negatively impacted, and you'll struggle to remember the information you have read. The result? You will not be in a position to perform at your best on the day of the test, and the original belief becomes a reality. You'll be reading more on beliefs in the next chapter.

So learning to dream again, to visualise what it is you deeply desire, will help shift the negative self-fulfilling prophecies into positive ones.

While we can use creative visualisation to focus on outer goals like a new car, a great job, or a passionate relationship, in reality, a purpose-filled and rewarding outer life relies on our having a rich inner connection to our soul, and our hearts desire. As Shakti Gawain, the master of creative visualisation teaches us in her book of the same name, happiness is about more than simply creating the material things that we want. It's about creating a life full of meaning, spiritual richness, and abundant joy. And don't we all crave that within our heart and mind?

Honestly, people who have used this technique regularly have been able to shift their lives in directions they didn't believe would be possible before they began to embrace the power of their conscious creative mind.

Some famous people who swear by the power of conscious visualisation, and have used it to improve their own lives and skills, are Arnold Schwarzenegger, Oprah Winfrey, and Jim Carey, to name just a few. As Oprah famously said, "Create the highest, grandest vision possible for your life, because you become what you believe." How true is that?

So creative visualisation is the ability to imagine an idea, and get a mental picture or a feeling of something you wish to manifest in your life. Then if you continue to focus on that idea regularly, imagining yourself achieving that end, seeing yourself in your mind's eye living the life you desire, and feeling it as if it were already true, chances are that you will actually achieve what you have been imagining.

Your dream can be experienced on many different levels – physical, emotional, mental or spiritual. You might imagine yourself in a new home, a fulfilling career, a successful business, or rewarding relationships with yourself and others, feeling deeply calm and content with life, and a deep inner peace.

You can also use this technique to support you when you're faced with a difficult situation, imagining yourself effortlessly managing a positive outcome in spite of the challenging circumstances. So you can work on many levels here, and by consistently imagining positive outcomes, your life will begin to open up to you in ways you never thought would have been possible.

Another process takes you through imagining yourself already having successfully achieved your dream life and diving deep into 'A Day in the Life you have dreamed of'. This technique is a very powerful tool to help you integrate all five senses – taste, touch, smell, sight, and hearing. Even if you think you can't see the vision or create a clear enough picture, or you close your eyes and maybe all you see are colours, or even just a blank screen, that's okay. The key here is to use any of the five senses. If you can't see your new job, business success or home – can you hear it? Imagine a conversation you could be having with someone expressing yourself with courage and confidence about your new life.

Why not you?!

Michael Jordan, the legendary basketball player said, "Every time I feel tired while exercising and training, I close my eyes to see that picture, to see that list with my name on it. This motivates me to work again."

And as Lindsay Vonn, the World Cup-winning skier said, "I always visualise the run before I do it. By the time I get to the start gate, I've run the race 100 times already in my head, picturing how I'll take the turns."

Powerful stuff right – so why not you? Why shouldn't you begin to believe in the power of conscious visualisation to create your dream life?

It doesn't matter if life has thrown you a complete curve ball, and you find yourself facing a completely different direction. You can begin from where you are right now, and start to use the power of your imagination to create the life you deeply desire. That way you'll get to write the next chapter of your life on your terms.

When Tom first had his accident and we were left shattered and lost, we couldn't trust ourselves to dream again. However now that we understand the power of our consciousness to create our lives, we use it all the time. Look at Tom, he first thought that life might never be great again, however he now lives in a beautiful home with his gorgeous wife and their beautiful little girl. They run an award-winning dog training business and are visualising a future where they support other people with spinal injuries to see that life can and will be amazing, if they just believe in themselves and their ability to dream.

So how do we begin this journey of conscious visualisation? Well, the technique is basically very simple.

Firstly, you need to find a quiet space where you won't be disturbed. Then begin to relax. You could use the guided meditation at the end of this chapter to help you get into a deep, quiet, meditative state of mind. Then begin to imagine yourself achieving a desired goal that you have set for yourself. You'll know you're on the right track if you trust your heart and imagination to show you the way.

Imagine yourself in the physical setting or environment that you would love to be in, doing work that you love, being in a supportive relationship, and living in a home that fills you with joy, or whatever your dream might be. It could be simply living with peace in your heart. Begin to see yourself telling others about this vision, and start to feel what it will feel like for you to already be experiencing the outcome you desire. Add in minute details like colours, smells, views, rewards, all the details that are important to you. Start to get a feeling in yourself that this is possible, and experience it as if it is really happening. In short, imagine it exactly the way you'd like it to be as if it were already the truth.

I encourage you to practice this short, simple exercise as often as you can, preferably each morning before you begin your day. If your vision is clear and you are focused on your intention to make it happen, then chances are you may begin to find a shift taking place in your life fairly quickly.

It is not necessary to believe in any metaphysical or spiritual ideas to use creative visualisation. You just need to be willing to entertain the idea that it is possibly for you to achieve whatever it is that you desire, and to have faith and hope that your power to dream can create a life you will love.

The one thing that is necessary though, is a desire to enrich your knowledge and experiences, and have an open mind to trying something new in a positive way. So if you practice the techniques, study the principles, and decide for yourself if they are useful for you, then you can go on to use, develop and expand them, and soon the changes in yourself and your life will definitely exceed anything you could have originally dreamed of.

As Shakti Gawain says in her book, "The process of creative visualisation is that at first, what might seem amazing or impossible to the very limited type of education our rational minds have received, will become perfectly understandable once we learn and practice the underlying concepts involved."

Once you get the hang of this and manage to do it successfully, it may seem like you are working miracles in your life…and you truly will be beautiful one!

By scanning the QR code, you can access a creative visualisation meditation I've recorded to guide you as you embark on this incredible journey. Remember – what we think about, comes about!

Here's to taking your first step toward uncovering what truly matters to you!

REFLECTION

This is an opportunity to begin practicing visualising your deepest desires. Simply follow the four steps below:

Step 1: Get Comfortable
Sit or lie down somewhere comfortable. Close your beautiful eyes and take a few moments to settle in.

Step 2: Breathe Deeply
Start breathing deeply, slowly, and naturally. Allow each breath to help you relax further into this moment.

Step 3: Relax and Let Go
Gradually release any tension in your body and let your mind ease into this peaceful space.

Step 4: Visualise Your Desire
In this relaxed state, begin to visualise what you deeply desire for your life. Imagine it as vividly and clearly as possible. This might seem difficult to begin with, but with practice you'll find your imagination all over again. Feel yourself in the moment, and visualise your surroundings as clearly as possible, what do you hear, smell, feel, see? Allow yourself to begin to imagine what it would be like for you if this desire was true.

Now that you know how to do it, I'd encourage you to practice this each morning before you begin your day. This simple yet powerful exercise will help you to open up to more joy, clarity and opportunity in every aspect of your life.

Man often becomes what he believes himself to be. If I keep on saying to myself that I cannot do a certain thing, it is possible that I may end by really becoming incapable of doing it. On the contrary, if I have the belief that I can do it, I shall surely acquire the capacity to do it even if I may not have it at the beginning.

MAHATMA GANDHI

STEP 2

CHAPTER 3

BELIEFS
Perception v Reality

How did you find the chapter on visualising your future?

Are you excited, and can you feel your 'why' getting stronger?

I understand how difficult it can be to believe in an exciting future when you have experienced a challenging event in your life.

That's why this chapter on beliefs is going to be so powerful for you. It's aimed at helping you to move past those thoughts that are holding you stuck and not supporting you anymore.

I'm passionate about the topic of beliefs because they shape the way we see the world.

I say that because beliefs serve as the lens through which we perceive the world and ourselves. They shape our thoughts, emotions, and actions, guiding us in navigating life's challenges and opportunities. However, not all beliefs are empowering; some may hinder our growth and success.

Our beliefs are often formed in response to our experiences, upbringing, and societal influences. They can be deeply ingrained within us, shaping our identity and worldview. While some beliefs empower us to pursue our goals with confidence and resilience, others may limit our potential and hold us back from realising our dreams.

And there you have it!

Often the reason we can't believe that we can trust our visualisations and desires is because our old beliefs are clouding our thoughts and perspective.

It took Tom's accident to rock my world and make me take stock of my own un-supportive beliefs, and ultimately change my life. I share this with you because it forced me to look long and hard at what really mattered to me. What's more, Tom's accident challenged me to understand why those things mattered. Getting to that point wasn't a simple or easy journey though. I went through a very dark place for many years, feeling like life had completely taken a sharp left turn, and I had no idea how to find my way forward again.

Ironically, while Tom courageously tried to adapt to his new reality, I found myself spiralling into despair. I entered a period where hope seemed elusive, and life felt devoid of purpose. I struggled to envision a positive future, unable to forgive myself for not being a better mother, wife, or friend. It was all very irrational, and I just couldn't find any gratitude or appreciate the blessings around me.

This chapter delves into my journey from this bleak mindset to a place of empowerment. I share this journey with you, not only to own my vulnerability, but to offer you a beacon of hope in the knowledge that there is light at the end of this very dark tunnel. I aim to guide you gently through this transformation, equipping you with the tools to maintain resilience and perspective even in the face of adversity.

My desire is for you to discover an empowering perspective that will support and guide you through whatever challenges life has to throw at you.

When I am asked how I survived the traumatic time I went through in 2012, I always say it was through a gradual process of reclaiming balance and well-being, one step at a time.

What's more, coming to terms with my own beliefs and transforming any of them that were not serving me anymore (if they ever did), was key to my ability to heal and find my purpose. What that led to was a beautiful period of consolidation of everything I'd learned in the process of finding my way back to myself, and discovering a deep passion for helping others to do the same.

That journey started with becoming consciously aware of what really mattered to me by identifying my inner values and priorities. And the key to that was waking up to the beliefs that were shaping the way I thought and behaved.

However, to begin this journey together now, we need to go back to basics and look at what beliefs are, where they come from, and the impact they have on our lives. By delving into our unconscious beliefs, we can begin to see how we have been creating a veritable glass ceiling that has been stopping us from reaching our full potential.

To break free of this default mode, we need to first identify those limiting beliefs, and then go on to learn how to change old patterns and create a supportive mindset that will enable us to achieve the life we desire.

That's what we need to do to be able to start living a life of purpose and opportunity again, and to move from those low-level thinking habits into nurturing, inspiring habits that will bring about more joy, hope and incredible opportunities we can't see when we are stuck in those dark places. In short, it's about moving into a more empowering mindset. This starts with understanding our limiting beliefs in order to be able to cultivate empowering ones. Then, tapping into the transformative power of awareness, and asking ourselves powerful questions in order to stay on track.

We are going to look at each of these components in a bit more detail now.

Understanding Limiting Beliefs:

As far as definitions go, a belief is an opinion or thought that we hold to be true. Beliefs are important because they impact our identity. I say that because they are at the core of how we see ourselves, what we think we are capable of, and what we understand to be true about ourselves and others.

The first step toward any change is to become aware of and challenge any limiting beliefs we may be holding onto. Examining our beliefs is important because we need to unearth our truth to be able to have the confidence and clarity we will need to make courageous decisions, expand our comfort zone, and take the actionable steps needed to move toward the life we have been visualising.

So I guess this is as good a time as any to say that one thing this will (or at least could) call on us to do, is get a bit uncomfortable as we grow and understand ourselves better.

If you've never done that before, trust me it can be truly eye opening. This is especially true if you're carrying the legacy of being a people pleaser around with you, or if you overthink everything and compare and judge yourself and others. Taking time to examine your beliefs is a critical strategy for you to get to a place where you can be who you really are at your core – i.e. incredible, creative, inspiring, compassionate and so much more.

The Transformative Power of Awareness:

Contrary to popular belief, our mindset is not fixed and can be changed over time with awareness. The power of awareness brings with it the clarity of mind we need to be able to identify what's not in alignment with who we really are. This encompasses everything from our thoughts, to the people we interact with, to the media we consume, what we read, and so on. This kind of awareness is a necessary precursor to being able to change the **de**structive stories from our past into **con**structive stories for our future, to move forward into a more fulfilling life – the one we have been desiring deep within.

A really helpful mindset shift in this regard that was paramount in my own journey, was the realisation that everything we've been through has actually happened FOR us and not TO us. When we change our perspective in this context, we are then able to become aware of the wisdom of our past experiences and begin to use this information for our personal growth and development. This then gives us the ability to take our lives to a whole other level.

Here's an interesting bit of information about conscious awareness, or should I say – the lack thereof. In every moment we are exposed to over two million pieces of information coming at us. We might have the TV blaring, music playing, the fan running, traffic noises, bird song, people talking and thoughts cluttering our subconscious 'awareness'. That said, we are only able to be conscious of a grand total of 7 pieces of information. The way we cope with that is by being very effective 'deleters'. That's an unconscious capacity we have to leave irrelevant stuff out.

If we didn't have this capacity, we would always be overloaded with a barrage of mental 'noise' triggered by everything going on around and within us.

Cultivating Empowering Beliefs:

The fact that we delete most of the sensory information we're exposed to, is an important piece of awareness in and of itself, but it's especially relevant here because it's our beliefs that determine what we notice and what we 'delete'. Or perhaps, rather than saying we delete some of the incoming 'information and sensations', a more apt way to put it is that we don't bring them to conscious attention. In other words, anything that confirms a belief we hold about ourselves or the world around us, is the thing that we're going to notice.

For example, when you think about a particular car you might like to buy, you suddenly see that car everywhere. I'm sure you're aware of that phenomena. It happens all the time, right!

Understanding this concept is crucial because it makes sense of the fact that our beliefs are shaping our perception of life. It explains why it is that what we think about comes about!

Don't get me wrong, there's effort involved in rewriting old programming. Remember it's been your default for a very long time. This insight perfectly explains why it takes effort to overwrite old patterns that no longer serve us.

What that involves is becoming aware of it when we have a disempowering thought, such as *I'm so clumsy* or *I've tried this before, why would it work now?* And then to stop and ask ourself – 'What purpose is that thought serving me?' If the answer is that it's not serving any purpose, then it's time to replace it with a more empowering thought, and focus on that until it becomes our default mode. The empowering thought could be something like 'I move with grace and ease'. At first, this is probably going to feel really un-natural, but given time it will become your new normal. Try it!

Also, delving deeper into our thought patterns can lead to the awareness of unconscious conditioned beliefs that may be holding us back. You know the ones – I'm too short, I'm too tall, I can't spell, I'm not pretty enough, I'm too pretty!

Basically, we all have beliefs that are based in insecurity or unworthiness. I like to think of them like sticky notes all over our back, occasionally we catch them in the mirror, and then by asking probing questions and persistently exploring these old patterns, we begin to uncover their origins. Often we wind up tracing them back to past traumas or experiences from our childhood that we have unconsciously held onto. The problem is that we believe them to be true, and as an adult we haven't stopped to re-examine them to see if they really are. Often when we do this simple yet powerful exercise, we realise that they are not our true beliefs at all, and we can begin to peel the sticky note away.

Powerful Questions to Ask Ourselves:

I have some really powerful questions I was asked during my own growth through a dark time that I know will be helpful for you on your journey to becoming aware of your own limiting beliefs.

When you notice you've thought something that is on the unsupportive side of the spectrum, you can start to turn things around by asking yourself – *How is this thought/belief supporting me?* Or *Why do I believe this thought to be true?*

If you just keep drilling down, you will often uncover what's really going on. This is so important because the issue around embedded fear (which is what underlies a belief like 'not being safe') could stem back to an experience we had when we were a child where we were traumatised in some way that has never been acknowledged or dealt with.

We can't go back in time, but what we can do is acknowledge what went on when we were little, remembering to apply lots of self-compassion in the process. And with support when we need it, we can do the work to heal the pain from the inner child that needs to be recognised and healed. That way we can get on with our lives unencumbered by past limiting beliefs around not being safe, or whatever it is in your case.

There is so much support for inner child healing available today. If you don't know where to start, you can check out the resource page on my website for more information.

For now though, I just want you to understand that by believing that you can let go of anything that no longer supports you, and reprogramming your brain by continuing to challenge and refute limiting beliefs whenever they emerge, you will literally rewrite the script that you're living your life by.

In my own case, I recently had an epiphany about a recurring phrase I often used unconsciously. That phrase is 'As if'. For example, 'As if that will ever work out for me', or As if I could really do that'. Do you have one or more of these sayings yourself?

Fortunately, I recognised the detrimental impact this seemingly harmless expression was having on me. It literally served as a subtle reminder of my limiting belief regarding my capacity to lead a fulfilling life aligned with my dreams and my purpose. This is the power of awareness in action.

After asking myself the question *Why do I believe this thought to be true?* it became evident that this inner dialogue stemmed from an outdated narrative rooted in my past experiences. Like everyone else, my past had been shaping my future. When I became aware of the internal dialogue, I set out to uncover its origins, and I realised that I had unwittingly absorbed someone else's beliefs from my past, allowing them to permeate my unconscious mind and shape my actions and perception of life. This revelation highlighted the need to confront and challenge these unconscious beliefs to reclaim control over my own life, if I was ever going to fully become the woman I knew I was within my heart. Now I have the supportive phrase I use whenever I feel like I need it that goes like this – 'Everything is always working out for me.'

So I'd like to turn the focus back on to you and get you to think about what old beliefs you have been holding onto that are stopping you from living a fulfilling life. This simple exercise in awareness is a very powerful way to bring your conscious mind into connection with your unconscious conditioned mind so that you can uncover a whole other world of opportunities. The beautiful thing is that when we become aware of our unconscious beliefs, we are 95% along the way to healing, changing, and mastering our mindset. That's the way to live life by choice and not by chance. And who wouldn't love to live like that?

A Scientific Twist

Okay, so I know that not everyone reading this book will necessarily agree that our beliefs shape how we see things yet. So for those who like to have things explained with a scientific twist, let's focus on how our brains work.

How often do we look for the negatives in our lives or a situation we're facing? It often seems like we immediately look for what's wrong, or we remember the negative parts of our past before the positive parts – would you agree? I certainly saw that pattern play out in my own life in the past. *So why is that,* you might ask. That's a great question. It's one I looked for the answer to on many occasions when I was feeling overwhelmed and lost.

So, let's explore that question with reference to our brain before we go any further, because there is actually a scientific reason why we 'react' instead of 'responding' to situations in an unconscious way a lot of the time. The reason is that deep in the centre of the brain is what neuroscientists call the limbic system. It holds the thalamus, the hippocampus, and the amygdala, which are all important in the context of the way we might default to negative patterns. Stay with me. It will all make sense soon.

Then there is the prefrontal cortex that is positioned at the front of the brain. It is the executive command centre which is sometimes called the logic centre of the brain. All of the sensory data, except in the case of smell, comes through the limbic brain via the thalamus which distributes that information to the prefrontal cortex and to the amygdala at the same time.

The amygdala consists of two little almond-shaped nodes that are like temperature gauges that give us a warning signal when we experience something that we have felt before and didn't enjoy. Essentially, it's job is to process sensory information and determine how we should respond emotionally to things that happen. For example – the memory of something that happened in the past triggers the amygdala to decide that there is something 'wrong' going on, and it redirects all of the data that was going to the prefrontal cortex (where it would have been logically worked through), to the emotional part of the brain. This then causes us to have an emotional reaction to the situation, instead of being able to apply a logical response.

Does that make sense? How amazing is that?

So you see there is a scientific reason why we react instead of responding to a challenging situation. Among other things, it explains why we have to help our brain by becoming aware of our emotions which are triggered by our beliefs. If we can start to become aware of our emotional reactions, we can begin to retrain our brain to respond in a more logical way, and this is how we overcome our limiting beliefs. For example, after Tom's operation in Perth, there came a time when everyone had to leave and get on with their lives, and it made sense that I should stay and support Tom in his recovery until he was well enough to be able to make the long journey home to Brisbane.

However, my limbic system was activated. I was on high alert all the time trying to ensure Tom received the best care and attention while I was feeling isolated and abandoned. On the physical level, I was overwhelmed and exhausted. Looking back on it all now, I can see that an old belief I carried around about my having to do everything on my own was both isolating and confusing me.

My mind slipped into the thought pattern that I had to do everything myself because I believed that asking for help equated to showing weakness. Finally (thank goodness) the penny dropped, and I realised that the truth was that people would always be there for me if I needed to reach out for help at any stage. I also accepted that it was totally reasonable for everyone who'd rallied around when Tom's situation was so scary, to eventually have to return to their homes and get on with their life.

I just shake my head, as well as feeling incredibly grateful, when I think about what a perfect storm Tom's accident was in terms of bringing my limiting beliefs to the fore. I say that because being stressed to the max meant that my amygdala was doing what it does – keeping me safe – and my worst fears were always front of mind. Luckily a sort of autopilot kicked in. That's what our nervous system does when our adrenals are on high alert. And mine were on high alert because everything I relied on to anchor my identity to (without being consciously aware of it, of course) had been taken away in an instant. I didn't even have the familiarity of my home to help me feel comfortable.

If I knew then what I know now about the interaction of mindset with physiology and life events, I would have focused on the comfort I got from my beautiful friend who was there and available to me all the time, and that I could reach out to if I ever wanted company or a shoulder to cry on. What's more, I had family and friends ringing every other day and continually holding a space for me. But I'm sorry to say that for way too long, the fact that I was being supported by people who cared about me went through to the keeper because I was obsessively worrying about Tom, and our future.

What I know now that I didn't know then, is that it was my conditioned beliefs that were triggering me, and pushing me into the trap of believing my thoughts, which enabled me to master the not so gentle art of catastrophising. With self-compassion and hindsight, I can now recognise that as well as being worried almost to death, I was sad and lonely and frightened about not being able to go the distance and keep 'doing it all' by myself.

The thing is that fear is a tricky emotion, and as I think back over what I went through with the wisdom of hindsight, I can remember only too well the way that fear often morphed into anger and other things like comparison and judgment. When I was at my lowest ebb, I was all but completely at the mercy of my unconscious conditioning where my itty bitty shitty committee was in overdrive.

Have you ever been in a situation where you felt like that when life has overwhelmed you, and you fall into believing your low-level thoughts are true? Well, let me tell you, you are not alone here, and it is often not your fault. It's a conditioned part of our brain, the survival mode, that has become a bully again and wants to remind you that you need to be careful. However, it is in these times when we need to question our beliefs and ask, "Is this thought supporting me right now?"

What I want you to understand is that there's nothing wrong with you if you've struggled when something you expected to turn out one way hasn't gone that way at all. The thing is that what's actually going on here is that your amygdala has been activated, and you're only able to see the world through your unconscious conditioned programming. That's when our thoughts in particular, and our perspective more generally, get skewed. I hope this makes sense. It certainly explained a lot to me in terms of why we unconsciously fall into believing the worst of a situation.

When the amygdala, which is like the emotional control centre in our brain, takes over, our logical thinking brain, the prefrontal cortex, goes on vacation. When this happens, instead of calmly working through things, our thoughts get stuck in the emotional part of our brain which isn't so great at keeping things in perspective.

For example, if you're feeling powerless, you might think, *I'm always stuck cleaning up after everyone else, and I'm tired of it.* But if you can pause and think about it, you might realise that there's another way you could see things. Maybe you could think, *I'm lucky to have people who rely on me, and I know that if I ask for help, they would be more than happy to support me.*

Now I don't know your exact situation, but if that second option sounds better to you, then changing your life starts with recognising those negative thoughts. Once you're aware of them, you can start training your brain to turn them around. Then instead of reacting to life, you can respond to it in a way that's emotionally healthy and empowering. Remember, knowing what's going on inside your head is key to feeling emotionally balanced.

We can re-train the amygdala to recognise that we feel safe and supported by constantly reminding ourselves that we are safe when those old feelings arise. This process is called the Sympathetic Reconditioning of the Amygdala.

I follow an incredible coach called Dr Claire Zammit PHD.

She's well known for the research she has done on what she calls the three hidden power blocks that stop conscious, caring people from creating a life that really matters to them. The three blocks in question are shame, lack, and isolation.

Shame is an underlying belief about who you think you are that may have been limiting your ability to fully create the outcome you want in any or all of the key areas of your life.

Lack is the feeling of being disconnected from yourself, from significant others, or from a higher power and a loving universe that's ready to support you. That higher power is tantamount to tapping into a deep source of wisdom, self-trust, courage, and the resilience that is already within you.

Isolation is more than just the experience of being alone, even though we might be surrounded by others. It's also about feeling isolated when it comes to creating the things that your heart is yearning to bring forward in your life, and actually becoming the person you came here to become.

Zammit found in her research that people who embody their own power deeply are much more likely to be able to make meaning out of their experiences, whether they are good or bad. Meanwhile, those who are at the mercy of the three hidden power blocks will be so busy blaming themselves or others for not being good enough that they fail to realise they are totally loveable and worthy, and that they have every right to be seen and heard.

I'd like to encourage you to take some time for yourself and reflect on this chapter about beliefs. It's not just about ticking a box; it's about giving yourself the space to truly delve into where you are now compared to where you desire to be.

I hope that if it does nothing else, this chapter leaves you with three powerful takeaways about your beliefs. They are:
- A clear understanding of how your current beliefs shape your life, and how aligning them with your aspirations can unlock new possibilities.
- A deep sense of self-compassion, recognising that growth is a journey, and it's okay to embrace where you are right now.
- The realisation that by challenging and reframing your limiting beliefs, you can unleash the limitless potential within you.

So, I want to encourage you to sit quietly and begin to examine your beliefs, language, and thoughts that might be holding you back from living your dream life. While there is an exercise on this coming up on the Reflections page you'll get to shortly, I thought it might be worth sharing what came up for me when I was asked *what I knew for sure* about myself and my strengths. My answer to that questions was that I know for sure that I am loved, why, because my children tell me this all the time, and when I let go of my ego and leant into this love, I knew for sure that it was true. Therefore, it follows that I am loving, I am loveable, and I am loved. Does that make sense? I promise you that putting in the effort to do this exercise and go on to evaluate and get rid of old patterns that aren't working for you can truly transform your life, business or career. And as you do that, you'll start to see joy and incredible opportunities unfold.

REFLECTION

This exercise is about exploring your beliefs and discovering how they shape your actions and goals. It's aimed at helping you to reflect on what comes up for you, and gain clarity about the beliefs that inform the decisions you make.

Step 1: Reflect on Your Beliefs
Finish the sentences that would follow the four points below, and observe what comes up for you. Among other things, this is an exercise in awareness and reframing a negative 'belief' by articulating what you know for sure about yourself and your abilities in a positive way.

☐ I can't: _____

Reframe

☐ I know for sure that I can: _____

☐ I'm not: _____

Reframe

☐ I know for sure that I am: _____

Step 2: Assess Your Beliefs
Ask yourself the following questions:

☐ Are my beliefs about myself true, or have I inherited them?

☐ What beliefs might be hindering me from achieving my goals?

Write your answers and thoughts below:

_____

_____

_____

_____

Step 3: Examine the Purpose
Consider what purpose the disempowering belief/s you identified in step 2 could be serving.

☐ Are they keeping me safe but stuck?

☐ Are they empowering me to grow?

Write your reflections below:

Step 4: Visualise Your Options Without Limits
If I changed my beliefs so that I knew I couldn't fail, how would I approach the question of achieving my deepest desires?

Sometimes we don't recognize our own strengths until we come face to face with our greatest challenges.

UNKNOWN

STEP 3

CHAPTER 4

ATTRIBUTES
Your inner strengths

Can you remember a time when you had to make a courageous decision? I'm sure that every single person reading this book will have had to make a courageous decision at some point in their lives. It's just not possible to get through life on this planet and not have to face a challenge or two. Would you agree?

In this chapter, we'll explore the question of what strengths and attributes are, and how we tap into our own inner strengths that are already within us. Even though there's every chance you may not be aware you have them, they will be there, supporting you to get through whatever life throws at you.

My desire for you as you're reading this chapter is to gain an awareness of the powerful qualities in the form of attributes that are uniquely yours. These attributes are there for you to access and lean into every day of your life. They can be incredibly reassuring and empowering. The thing about attributes is that they are not just available to you when you find yourself in a challenging situation. Certainly, they are particularly important when it comes to overcoming challenges, however learning to tap into and utilise them to achieve your full potential is the key to literally changing the trajectory of your life.

So what is an attribute you may ask? The Oxford Dictionary explanation states – "An Attribute is a quality, feature or characteristic that is an **inherent** part of who we are." Therefore, your strengths and attributes are already within you. You are born with a set of unique strengths and attributes designed to support and nurture you to achieve your specific life purpose and whatever challenges and surprises arise along your journey. They are inherent within you.

Jo Britto is the author of "The Six Attributes of a Leadership Mindset" which focuses on leadership in relation to professional development within organisations and businesses. I love what he has to say about growing our mindset and developing positive behaviours, it's about leading ourselves, and by example, leading others to achieve better outcomes than they would otherwise achieve.

The attributes he identifies as being important to our growth are Mindfulness; Genuine Curiosity; Flexibility of Mind; Creating Leaders, and Enterprise Thinking.

He describes **Mindfulness** as the ability to be present so that we can see what's really going on under the surface of a situation. That's important because being able to make decisions based on what's actually going on, rather than relying on a one-dimensional view of what's happening at any given time, will make a big difference to the way our life pans out.

Genuine Curiosity manifests itself when we ask ourselves questions that will help us to understand why we do the things we do. Remember Step 2, where we looked at how our old beliefs can cloud our perception of life. The topics you're reading about and the questions I'm asking you to pause and reflect on throughout this book, are all about becoming curious.

Flexibility of Mind involves three parts. These are recognising that we could be wrong (hard I know, lol); understanding that there will be more than one solution to any problem, and exercising the ability to creatively combine the solutions into what Britto calls 'a revolutionary idea'.

When he talks about **Resilience,** Britto goes back to basics and uses words like 'keeping on keeping on', and 'getting back up after we've been knocked down', which we can do by tapping into our inherent attributes and strengths.

Creating Leaders is about having or developing qualities that inspire others to think for themselves. I actually had a bit of a watershed moment with this point because I never thought of myself as a Mindset leader until the person who edited this book for me pointed out that there was no doubt in her mind that I was. What she said was that from where she sat, inspiring readers to become the leaders of their own lives and beyond is exactly what this book is all about.

WOW! It just goes to show that opportunities to deepen our self-awareness are everywhere.

Last but not least there is **Enterprise Thinking**. Britto's focus is on individuals working together to do what is best for the business because they understand that by doing so, they are benefiting the enterprise as a whole. In a broader sense, I feel like taking an alternative perspective here, what if we saw our life as a 'business' and by putting the work into creating the best version of ourselves, we literally invest in creating a successful, happy life that creates a ripple effect out into our marriages; families; friendships; work environments, and community!

I absolutely love that concept. It's been called a 'Benefits Mindset' which builds on the idea of a 'Growth Mindset' that entails an appreciation of the fact that our abilities can be developed, rather than being fixed. It goes one step further though because it includes the notion that we should focus on living with a more caring, inclusive and interdependent perspective. The bottom line here is that we all need to take responsibility for creating the world we'd love to live in, by taking responsibility for our own emotional wellbeing, and caring about the wellbeing of others.

Inspiring Strengths

When I think about inherent strengths and attributes, I am reminded of the many people I met at Shenton Rehabilitation Centre when Tom was moved out of the emergency ward in Perth. We met so many courageous men and women who'd had their lives completely turned upside down on an ordinary day, and yet found their own inner strength to keep going and make the best out of their situation, not just with sheer will, but an inner strength that was inspiring to see.

I met a beautiful man whose name was Jack in Tom's ward. He was like a father figure and a guiding light to me in those challenging times. He was in his early 80s when he tripped on the corner of his bed and hit his head on the bedside table breaking his neck – can you imagine what that would be like? The fact that this didn't stop Jack from making the most out of a bad situation, or his enthusiasm for living the best life he possibly could was just astounding.

It's no overstatement to say that the way Jack supported me was my saving grace. He was an amazing man on so many levels. His background included coming to Australia from the UK during the Second World War and living in a boarding school from the age of 10. He had to make his own way in life. One day when I was feeling particularly overwhelmed, he said "Chris, life is like a tapestry, woven with threads of many colours. Those threads show up in the form of amazing memories. Some we'd like to forget. Some bring us joy. Some are dark and challenging, but all of the threads are part of a beautiful unique story we call our life. That story is about how we use our strengths to rise and rise again and see life as the incredible tapestry that it is."

Even though Jack was a quadriplegic at 80-something, he still saw the beauty in life, and in people like Tom and myself, and shared that love from his heart with all those around him.

Jack and his wife Peggy planned to travel back to England once Jack got better, but unfortunately, he passed away before that happened. When Peggy rang to tell me about his passing, she said that he never forgot about Tom and me and the love and support we gave him. It's lovely that he felt that way, but trust me, from where I sit it was the other way around in terms of who supported who.

If Jack is looking down on us, I want to say "Thank you, Jack. You may be gone but you will never be forgotten. You will be in my heart forever you beautiful man."

I share Jack's story with you because when it comes to talking about our inherent attributes and strengths, I can't think of a better case study to share with you than him.

I feel like the attribute that defines Jack more than the many positive ones he clearly had, is courage. Did you know the word courage is a derivative of 'Cor', which is the Latin word for heart? Courage originally meant to speak one's mind by telling all of one's heart. Jack certainly shared his heart with me, and I saw his courage on display when he was working as hard as he could to get the best possible result out of the rehab phase he was going through when we met.

So, I ask again, can you remember a time when you had to make a courageous decision? Think of the strengths or attributes that rose to the surface that helped you to expand your comfort zone and take the steps necessary to achieve the best possible result you could.

As with all of the chapters that cover the six steps of my ***BecomingYou*** journey, at the end of this chapter you'll find the Reflection page to consolidate what you've learnt in the process of reading the material in this chapter. In this case though, I'd encourage you to take a moment to write down what comes up for you in the process of delving into your past to answer the question I posed above now. I'm recommending this because as simple as this exercise might seem, it could well turn out to be a powerful reminder of what is true within you. The thing is that the strength that rises up within us when we make courageous decisions is a reflection of the inherent quality that is unique to us, and is supporting us to get through every day of our life.

Another deceptively simple exercise is to think about some of the qualities about yourself that you know to be true. What I'm referring to here are things like Tenacity, Persistence, Passion, Compassion, Humour, Creativity, Strategic thinking, Loyalty, and anything else that comes up.

This is important because when we become aware of our inner strengths and attributes, we can take our results to a whole other level by leaning into them, owning them, and rising into our greatness. At the same time, we can start to let go of feeling isolated as we move through our journey, and realise that we can and will survive anything that life throws at us when we understand our unique, inherent attributes.

That's not to say that we will be totally immune to things like overwhelm and exhaustion. What it means is that awareness of our inner strengths will ensure that we have the tenacity and courage to never give up, and to rise above the itty bitty shitty chatter that is part of the survival mode that's programmed into our brains.

Change Your Ending

Just think of all of the fantastic examples of people who've literally started life over after experiencing a potentially soul-destroying event by coming out the other side even bigger and better than before, with the fire in their belly to make the world a better place.

For me, the 2015 Australian of the Year **Rosie Batty**, who turned her pain into her passion after her son Luke was killed by his father in 2014, is the first person who comes to mind. Rosie's legacy is the fact that there is now much more protection for victims of domestic violence and their children than there has ever been before in Australia where we are both based.

Then there's **Nathan Pitt** who was just an ordinary kid, when in 2015 he was returning home from a military training exercise as a 20 year old cadet when the bus he was travelling on rolled while taking a bend. Nathan was trapped underneath the bus for two long hours with critical injuries. It was the fast thinking of the other cadets travelling with him that saved his life. Among other things, they helped him stay focused on surviving until emergency teams arrived. His life was changed in an instant as he saw his dream of becoming a pilot go out the window when he was told his arm would need to be amputated. However, once Nathan began to recover and take the arduous rehabilitation steps forward, he used his he attributes including a positive mindset, and life began to open up again for him. Among other things, he did gain his pilot's license, and he represented Australia in the Invictus Games. For somebody who never thought they'd ever represent Australia in sport before his accident, Nathan literally turned his life around.

Similarly, **Turia Pitt** who suffered burns to 65% of her body in a grassfire that sprang up during an ultra-marathon in Western Australia's Kimberley region, turned her adversity into a book called "Everything to Live for". She also runs a podcast called "What do we learn about ourselves from doing hard things?" and has helped 40,000 people (and counting) through her digital courses. But it doesn't stop there – she's actually shared a stage with Tony Robbins, competed in the Ironman World Championships, sailed a boat around French Polynesia, and walked the Kokoda Trek.

Closer to home, a friend of mine called Kris who was a single mum supporting a son with a disability joined a dragon boating team and at the age of 58 travelled to Hungry for the World titles where her team won three Gold Medals. I feel like that's no mean feat for anyone in their 50s, but it's a tremendous achievement for a person like Kris who'd never even been sporty when she was a kid.

Tom Ross whose story you now know, married his sweetheart Maddie in 2017, won an interstate business award in 2019 for their unique dog training business called Beacon Dog Training on the Gold Coast, and is now the proud father to Bethany Christine who was born in 2022. And although every day can be a challenge with a Spinal Cord Injury (SCI), Tom's determination to live life as the best dad, husband, and businessman that he can be is nothing short of inspirational. His next venture is about inspiring other people with spinal cord injuries by his example of the fact that life can be fulfilling and complete no matter what legacy of the adversity we've gone through we might be carrying.

Take a moment now to consider someone you admire, and think about the admirable attributes they demonstrate. I'm asking you to do this because what we admire in others is often a reflection of our own inner qualities.

I shared the examples of people I find inspirational with you because

I want you to know that you can start from exactly where you are right now, and change the ending of your journey. The way to do that starts with understanding what your inherent strengths and attributes are.

The individuals I highlighted demonstrated that nothing is beyond reach, and age should never be a barrier to reigniting those dormant passions that lie within each of us. Transitioning from having an idea, to taking action can be daunting though. I say that because it often requires stepping out of our comfort zone. However, when we embrace our inherent attributes and lean in, we find that life steps up and supports us along the journey.

Taking the time to unearth your inherent attributes will change your life. I guarantee it.

REFLECTION

Take a moment to consider someone you admire, and write down three attributes about them you can also see in yourself. As I said earlier – what you see in others is often a reflection of your inner strengths!

_____

_____

_____

_____

Remember a time in your life when you persevered through a difficult time. What strength rose up within you?

_____

_____

_____

_____

_____

Do not be afraid to raise your standards. The right people and opportunities will always meet you where you are.

MANDY HALE

STEP 4

CHAPTER 5

STANDARDS
Your Secret Weapon

Let's take a moment to celebrate what you have unearthed so far, and recap the last three steps you've come through on this journey.

We began by focusing on starting with the end in mind through conscious visualisation, allowing ourselves to envision what we truly want to achieve, and clarifying our WHY for taking on this journey.

Next, we explored the barriers that often hold us back from those desires – our limiting beliefs and negative self-talk. We learnt how to begin reframing those thoughts, empowering ourselves to cultivate a mindset that nurtures and supports us.

Then, we unearthed our inherent strengths which are our natural attributes that can guide us through life's challenges, and support us through this journey.

Now let's dive into our standards. You might not have ever thought of yourself and your standards in the context we're talking about them here. In fact, you might not have realised that you have standards as such, but in this chapter you will identify your non-negotiable standards – those 'must' and 'must nots' that guide your life. You'll become aware of what's working well for you and what might be holding you back. You'll also learn how to raise any standards that no longer align with the person you are, and how to commit fully to living life on your terms through the new, supportive standards you set, or the ones you already have but aren't consistently honouring.

It's crucial to reflect on what you're allowing into your life, and consider whether your standards are helping or hindering your journey through this life you're living right now. Knowing whether you are setting the bar too low or too high in certain areas of your life, and then committing to doing something about it, is a very powerful exercise.

So, what do your standards look like in areas such as your business, relationships, and health?

As you've pondered that question, some of you might have realised that like many people, you are a part of the 'Should Club'. Do you ever hear the little voice in your head saying – *I should do this*, or *I should fix that*, or *I should start that fitness challenge*. We've all been there. However, because you're reading this chapter rather than skipping over it, I believe you want to raise your standards when it comes to supporting your life, including your business, career, emotional well-being, and the other components that make you uniquely you.

The stronger and clearer you make your standards, the more successful your ability to reach your goals will be. So I'm going to ask you some questions that will help you to discover and/or elevate your standards.

Remember, your standards are not just 'shoulds' – they are your 'musts'. These reflect the actions that are essential for keeping your life on track. Honouring your standards means acknowledging excuses when they arise, but refusing to let them dictate your actions, or lead to inaction. By staying true to your standards, you'll ensure the progress you make is in alignment with your goals.

Let's begin this journey by recognising a standard you're proud of right now.

- Do you take care of your health through mindful eating and exercising?

- Is your self-care a non-negotiable for you?
- Do you have a morning routine that sets you up with a positive tone for your day?
- Do you have strong boundaries in the different areas of your life, business or career?

If you haven't identified anything yet, that's okay – you're not alone. In fact, this can be an exciting place to start because it means there's so much potential for growth. By leaning into this chapter, you'll open yourself up to discovering meaningful insights that could make a big difference in your journey.

Sometimes, reframing a question can help your subconscious mind engage more deeply. For example, instead of berating yourself for making a decision that went against your standards, try asking yourself: *How often do I feel like I'm not meeting my own standards? And how does that make me feel?* Approaching it this way invites reflection without judgment.

Reflection

The truth of it is that many of us fall short when it comes to the standards we set for ourselves, whether it's how we care for our bodies, nurture our minds, cultivate relationships, or pursue our goals. If we don't prioritise high standards for our own wellbeing and the way we live, we risk moving through life on autopilot. It may sound like a cliché, but every choice we make shapes the life we create.

Take a moment to reflect on the standards you're currently living by in key areas of your life, including self-care, work or passion projects, relationships, growth, business, and career. Where might there be room to raise the bar?

Self-Care: Are you nourishing your body with healthy food and restorative practices? Do you make time to rest, recharge, and truly tune in to what you need?

Work or Passion Projects: Are you fully present for the things that matter most to you? Are you pursuing your goals with a clear intention and genuine effort?

Relationships: Are you fostering meaningful connections and setting boundaries that protect your energy? Are you surrounding yourself with people who uplift and support you?

Growth: Are you seeking opportunities to learn, evolve, and become your best self?

Business: Are you holding consistent standards for success in your business?

Career: Are you reliable, supportive, and inclusive in your professional life? Are you embracing your role with enthusiasm and a desire for continual learning?

As you reflect on these areas, consider where a small shift in your old well-worn perspective could lead to significant positive changes.

No matter how things are looking for you now, imagine raising your standards in these areas and consider how it would feel to show up for yourself in a way that your future self will thank you for.

Take exercise for example: Could you commit to moving your body in ways that keep it strong, flexible, and energised? Could you make it a non-negotiable part of your life to do the things you know will maintain or increase your fitness, instead of letting it slide to the bottom of your priorities all of the time?

Or how about relationships: What would change if you focused on creating deeper, more intentional connections? And in the world of work and/or learning, could you set bigger, bolder goals and ask for the support you need to achieve them?

Now, let's balance reflection with celebration. Take a moment to write down three things you're proud of when it comes to the standards you're already holding in your life.

This is important because your standards are the foundation for the life we want to create, and they are the cornerstone of everything we do. They shape the way we show up for ourselves, how we engage with others, and how we navigate our day to day existence. Remember, our thoughts create our emotions, and our emotions dictate how we show up in the world.

In other words, what we think about comes about!

For many, prioritising oneself before others can feel really uncomfortable. Yet, if you don't invest in your own well-being, growth, and clarity first, you won't have the energy, focus, or capacity to succeed when it comes to feeling fulfilled. What's more, when you commit to yourself, you'll be sending a powerful message to those around you. That message is that you value your time, energy, and purpose, and as a result, others will learn to value and respect you too. That's the ripple effect in action!

On the other hand, allowing the demands of the outside world to dictate your choices and chew up your energy is likely to leave you feeling scattered and reactive. I say that because without clear standards, you'll find yourself striving to meet unrealistic and possibly irrelevant expectations, simply because you haven't communicated your boundaries.

Raising your standards and standing firm in them gives you the strength and the focus required to align your actions with your goals, protect your intentions, and honour the vision you have for your life. Honesty plays a key role here, because living life on purpose entails saying what you mean, and meaning what you say. This isn't about being harsh or unkind; it's about being authentic.

For example, instead of defaulting to what others expect from you, you could calmly express your needs by saying something like, *Thank you for sharing that, however I feel...* This kind of simple honest communication shows others that you respect yourself. When that's the case, you'll find that they will be far more likely to respect you in return.

Clear boundaries are essential for protecting your time, energy, and well-being. Without them, others may unintentionally or intentionally ask more of you than you're comfortable giving, which can leave you feeling overwhelmed, resentful, or even drained. Over time, this can lead to things like frustration, burnout, or anger.

However, when you honour your standards and set healthy boundaries, you'll take back control of your life. You'll create space to live with intention, guided by your own inner compass. This is the foundation for a life filled with joy, fulfilment, and meaningful success.

Let's take a moment to reflect now. Think about your current personal standards in all areas of your life and consider –

- Where are your standards helping you to thrive?
- Where might they be holding you back?

In the Reflection section at the end of this chapter, you'll be writing down three personal standards or habits that no longer align with the person you have become. The important question here, is how can you begin to turn them around.

This simple exercise is an important step toward becoming aware of what really matters to you, and realigning the way you're living your life to achieve your true potential. When we genuinely take the time to examine our old standards, we begin the process of changing our mindset. What's great about that, is that you'll begin to see what's not working, and start to practice a conscious awareness that will help you to put the standards in place that are going to support you to have the life that will fill your heart with hope, clarity and incredible synchronicity. Essentially, you will begin to embrace what's possible.

Sometimes it helps to look inward and honestly examine the parts of ourselves we tend to avoid – those hidden habits, traits, or behaviours that are holding us back from achieving our full potential. These can often reveal areas where we've unconsciously set low standards.

Raising our Standards

How can you identify an old standard that no longer supports you? The answer to that question lies in the knowledge that a low standard is reflected in behaviours, habits, or mindsets that hold you back from being your best self. Take a moment to reflect and consider the following questions:

- Are your current standards truly acceptable to you?
- Do you allow others to let you down without addressing it? How does that make you feel?

- Are you showing compassion and respect for others, especially those facing greater challenges?

Acts of kindness, no matter how small – like never parking in a disabled spot, offering help to someone in need, or holding space for a silent prayer – can create ripples of positive change. Reflecting on this point, and the three questions you considered before it, can help you to recognise where perhaps the standards you have been living by have been limiting your opportunities to grow.

It can be tempting at times to find fault in others or engage in gossip, but it's worth considering how that affects our energy. The next time you're drawn into a gossip session, I'd encourage you to try pausing and instead, consider these alternatives: speaking directly to the person you have an issue with; talking to someone who can help resolve it, or simply walking away. I can assure you that taking a constructive approach will feel much more empowering and productive than venting without a solution being achieved.

Similarly, putting yourself down – whether to appear humble or as a defence mechanism – doesn't inspire respect. On the contrary, it diminishes your sense of self-worth and the esteem you're held in my others. Also, when someone offers you a compliment, practice gratitude. You can significantly raise your standard by simply thanking someone for a compliment, rather than making a self-effacing comment in an attempt to appear humble.

Dishonesty, even with ourselves, is a subtle yet limiting low standard. This matters because avoiding responsibility for our actions, or making excuses for not doing what's in our best interest, can hinder our growth. True integrity comes from owning our choices, embracing accountability, and learning from our experiences.

I'd like to encourage you to commit to adopting higher standards by:
- Making respect for yourself and others a non-negotiable priority.
- Prioritising your well-being – physically, mentally, and emotionally – in ways your future self will thank you for.
- Aligning your actions with your core values and the life you want to create.

Please take a moment to consider the following question, as you'll explore it more deeply in the Reflection section at the end of this chapter.

- What are three new non-negotiable standards you can commit to today to elevate your life, business, and career?

When you start living up to these higher standards, remember to celebrate yourself. I want to stress this because so often we go through life never stopping to acknowledge the effort we're putting in and the progress we're making on our emotional well-being journey. Too often, we focus on our mistakes or what we think we're doing wrong. This only drains our momentum and convinces us that we're not capable of change. If we want or expect others to acknowledge our changes and achievements when we haven't even done that for ourselves, we are often sorely disappointed.

Things will start to shift when you become your own biggest supporter. I'd love you to be able to see the beauty within yourself and get comfortable celebrating your achievements.

Shifting your focus to what you're doing right starts with noticing the small but meaningful steps you're taking, such as:

- The projects or tasks you've completed at work or in your business
- The connections you've strengthened in your personal and professional life
- The healthy choices you're making for your body and mind
- The moments you've spent reflecting, learning, or growing
- The way you're feeling more aligned with your goals.

Make no mistake about it, these small wins are the building blocks of your success and should not be overlooked. They show that you have a growth mindset and that is a very powerful asset.

The Ripple Effect

You see, your success really does matter. When you choose to create positive change in your life it will inspire and uplift others around you. This is because by cultivating realistic standards, you'll set an example and create a ripple effect of positivity in your life, business, and career. How wonderful would it be to share your life with others who are raising their own standards because you committed to yourself and your dreams for a beautiful life first?

So I encourage you to keep your focus on progress, not perfection, and fully commit to yourself and the life you deserve to be living.

This is not just about meeting goals. It's about creating a new benchmark for the way you show up for yourself and others. When you commit to higher but realistic standards, you'll begin to align

This is not just about meeting goals. It's about creating a new benchmark for the way you show up for yourself and others. When you commit to higher but realistic standards, you'll begin to align with the best version of yourself, unlocking opportunities, increasing your sense of fulfilment, and laying the foundation for lasting success.

I understand that embracing these new standards will require some willpower and discipline on your part, and I also understand that it can feel uncomfortable to begin with, however given time and patience with ourselves we can and will make a difference, not just in our own lives, but in the lives of those around us.

Think of Tom, learning all the new skills required to live life as a paraplegic, or anyone facing a life-changing event of any kind. They all had to find or change their standards to empower themselves to live the best life possible for them given their new circumstances. So, yes, a level of discipline is required. Basically, in this context, discipline can be described as consistently taking action toward what matters most, regardless of how we feel in the moment. It is the hallmark of excellence, and one of the foundational pillars of freedom.

I trust this is all making sense. The foundational pillar of freedom I mentioned above happens when we take control of our mindset, which results in our beginning to experience a level of joy and happiness that may have totally eluded us in the past. The truth is that while our feelings are valid, they don't always align with our long-term goals.

How often do we let fleeting emotions dictate our actions, holding us back from being able to make progress? It's a habit many of us fall into, myself included. What I want to stress here though, is that we actually have the power to change our mindset, and by committing to change in ways that increase our overall happiness, we are taking control of our journey and creating the life we truly desire.

This journey is about making intentional choices that reflect our deep desires in every aspect of our life. Whether it's showing up for our career with integrity, fostering meaningful relationships, or making time for personal growth, the effect of raising our standards will ripple through all of the areas of our lives.

So, which option will you choose moving forward? Will you let temporary feelings of uncertainty and a habit of avoiding discomfort dictate your actions, or will you commit to the discipline and consistency needed to build the life you desire?

This decision is paramount to living life by design – not by default.

You see, so many people give up on themselves when change requires them to get a little uncomfortable for a while and stretch their comfort zones, and to take actionable steps. So it really is those who persist, get up when they fall, and keep moving forward, who will find that life really is here to be enjoyed and not just something we struggle through.

The fact that you're here now shows that you've already made a choice, and that you have a growth mindset. You've taken significant steps toward growth, and you should be proud of the progress you've made. Whether progress ultimately plays out via a fitness challenge, a pivotal project in your career or business, or personal breakthroughs in your relationships, you've proven that you have what it takes to rise to your new standards.

Setting realistic, supportive standards isn't just about achieving success though. It's about discovering the truth of who you are and what really matters to you. Your standards serve as the compass guiding you toward a life of hope, clarity and abundant opportunity. They are your secret weapon.

Remember that your standards reflect your self-worth. When you set and live by them, you're not just creating a better life, you're uncovering the essence of who you truly are.

As if that wasn't incentive enough to take the matter of standards seriously, the fact is that when we change our standards, we tell the world that we are ready to receive all the abundance that she has to offer us. Then watch in wonder as life shows us new opportunities, unexpected joys, and the power of living in alignment with our true self.

REFLECTION

What are three personal standards you're living with that you know are not supporting you at the moment?

_____

_____

_____

_____

What are three new non-negotiable standards you can commit to today to elevate your life, business, or career?

_____

_____

_____

_____

What will have to change in order for you to abide by the new standards you are setting?

What will life look and feel like for you when you begin to live by your new standards?

*When you expect the best,
you release a magnetic force in your
mind that draws the best to you.*

Norman Vincent Peale

STEP 5

CHAPTER 6

EXPECTATIONS
Whose Are They Anyway

Our standards and expectations are shaping our world. They can be uplifting and supportive, or they can be literally sapping us of our essence.

An expectation is a strong belief that something will happen.

It is important to take account of this because our internal world determines the way our lives play out. I say that because expectations of ourselves and others play a crucial role in shaping our behaviours, goals and sense of achievement.

In this chapter we will explore whether our expectations of ourselves and others are realistic or unrealistic, and we'll look into how we break the cycle of expecting unrealistic outcomes.

When we take an honest moment to examine our expectations, we often find out that they are not even ours, or they are so high that we are always setting ourselves and others up for failure. Can you relate to that?

Every day, even every hour, we are consciously and unconsciously setting expectations of ourselves and others, especially those who are closest to us. These unconscious, unexamined and often unexpressed standards and expectations are dangerous. I say that because they will undoubtedly turn into a degree of disappointment we will feel in relation to ourselves and others.

Think about it, how often have you been disappointed with someone, and yet on reflection if you are honest with yourself, you can see that you played a big part in the outcome because you failed to fully express your expectations or standards with them? You are not alone.

Tiger Singleton, who is a thought leader I follow on Insight Timer, compares our unexpressed expectations to holding others prisoner in our own minds. When we let go of needing others to validate or see us in a certain way, we release ourselves from the constant pressure of judgment and comparison which is all in our mind. This notion is very powerful.

If we have unrealistic expectations of others, we can get the impression that they have let us down! And yet, on reflection, it's obvious that we consciously or unconsciously set them up to fail.

This pattern often leads to unnecessary disappointment and discord in relationships, causing feelings of shame, hurt, and even anger. Before my breakdown, which was a turning point that ultimately inspired the work I do today, I was unconsciously setting myself and others up for failure on a regular basis. The emotions I placed too much trust in took a significant toll on me and the quality of my relationships. I'm deeply grateful to have become more aware of these unconscious thoughts.

Taking the time to reflect on what truly matters to us allows us to find the courage to express ourselves honestly and advocate for our own needs.

Can you relate to my example in any way? I'm sure you can think of a time when something similar has happened to you either in your family or work environment.

In Brene Brown's book *Atlas of the Heart*, she explains that disappointment leads to feeling bad about ourselves and the other people in our life. Our negativity is tinged with astonishment and surprise, and, at the same time as we are trying to forgive, we've concealed our emotions. We're trying to think positively and urging ourselves to move on. It's really exhausting. I speak from experience here.

It doesn't have to be big stuff that leads to this state. Self-deprecating small talk is just as damaging to our unconscious fragile minds as being bullied in the schoolyard is. When we make comments like *Oh silly me*, or *You're so unco Chris* or *I'm so stupid – I'm always saying the wrong thing*, they are heard and interpreted by our unconscious mind, and made into beliefs we hold to be true about ourselves.

For example, let's say you're doing something that feels challenging, like putting together a flat-packed piece of furniture (God forbid) and you realise that you've screwed a piece in the wrong way around. How do you 'naturally' respond? Do you call yourself an idiot, or perhaps someone else does, and you accept their assessment as truth?

Or you find yourself walking out of a meeting of some kind, perhaps it's an interview. Do you find yourself turning your responses over and over again in your head – questioning and berating yourself as more and more doubts start creeping in. You're plagued by thoughts like – *Why did I say that? What made me think I could deliver the goods? How could I have been so stupid? Why would they want me?*

No matter what you do or say, you are never good enough in your own eyes. You are too slow, too clumsy, too old, too – you name it, and you wind up getting angry and impatient with yourself.

You have a list of unfulfilled ambitions. But you are doing nothing with them apart from using them to prove that you are a failure.

Do you generalise too? Oh gosh so many of us do this until we realise how toxic it can be to turn the belief that *I'm no good at* ....., to being *I'll **never** be any good at*...., or worse still, *I'm no good at anything!* So it's important to be on the lookout for words like 'always' or 'never' creeping into the statements you make about yourself or the situation you are in.

Another habit to watch out for (and address early) is saying *I set my standards very high.* While this may sound like a commendable sentiment, it often turns you into your own harshest critic, setting yourself up for inevitable disappointment. When you constantly impose unrealistic demands and unreachable expectations, you become an impossible taskmaster for whom nothing is ever good enough. Who needs enemies when you have yourself relentlessly driving a cycle of self-criticism?

It's a bit of a chicken and egg scenario we're dealing with here. I say that because this behaviour is disastrous for our self-esteem, and in turn low self-worth leads to more self-inflicted unkindness. This is something I call a 'with-holding of love' from ourselves, or to others. You know the ones, *I'll love you when you do such and such, I'll be happy when.., If only you were more like ...., If you just did as I asked I'd be happy*, or *I'll be happy when I lose weight* – and on it goes. You with-hold love in the mistaken belief that this will make you work harder, or the other person will try harder to please you.

Can you relate to this? We all do it to some degree or other.

The bottom line is that the cost of looking for perfection will only destroy our creativity and vitality – both in ourselves and others because of the knock-on effect it has on the emotional state we turn up with when we're interacting with the people in our lives.

No one is perfect. Everyone has flaws, and everyone makes mistakes. That's a fact. And that's okay.

Your expectations are what you anticipate an outcome to be. Personal expectations are the internal standards you set for yourself, therefore your personal expectations are what you plan to measure your own success or failure by. The thing is that we see our expectations as facts. and they become part of our belief system. We will have developed some of these from our experiences in life, and others could have been picked up from role models, peers or our parents.

This is an important point because the way we manage the interaction between our self-esteem and personal expectations will impact our approach to life. It will moderate our behaviour and our attitude in life, as well as our willingness to try new things, and thus our ability to develop and learn as well as we should be able to.

Unrealistic expectations will also have an impact on our mood. If our expectations are so unrealistic that they are unattainable, we will always feel worthless and consider ourselves to be a failure.

So it's important to set realistic goals, intentions and expectations. That's not to say that you shouldn't challenge yourself to raise the bar with the view to continuous improvement, but if we set the bar ridiculously high so that jumping over it is simply impossible, we run the risk of setting ourself and others up for failure.

Can you recognise an unhealthy expectation in your own life?

Do you sometimes wonder why you are not doing or being more when you know you should be?

The answer is always the same. It's because you never expect more of yourself. Or you feel too comfortable or scared to just 'go for it', and achieve one of those big hairy audacious goals we're likely to see others going on to achieve. It's an attitude that values playing it safe above all else that keeps us stuck in a place of lack.

Personal Expectations:

Below I've listed some key signs that suggest patterns of unrealistic expectations are at play:

- You feel stressed and upset when things don't go as planned or your routine deviates slightly
- You find plenty to criticise in yourself and others
- You fixate on small details and believe it is really important to get everything right
- When things go wrong, even in minor ways, you feel let down or frustrated
- You have very specific visions of how things should be and find it difficult to accept other outcomes
- You feel irritated and resentful when others don't fall in line with your plans.

It's normal to feel all of these things from time to time, however, if they play a recurring role in your life, it may be time to rethink your expectations and get help to move forward if you feel like you need it.

Expectations often stem from visions other people have for you. You might absorb these and carry them forward, even if they don't align with your dreams and desires. Now that you've learned a bit more about how expectations work, I encourage you to consider the expectations you may have unconsciously set by asking yourself whether they truly resonate with you. And then go further by considering whether achieving those expectations would fulfil you and bring you joy. This is a powerful question to stop and ask yourself.

When we have experienced a life-changing challenge, or we have reached a crossroads, or we have been confronted with an opportunity that would require us to stretch ourselves and our capabilities, it's not uncommon to feel vulnerable. To quote Brene Brown on this point – "Vulnerability is not a weakness; it's our greatest measure of courage."

It takes tremendous courage to show up as our authentic selves in a world where social media often presents an unrealistic lens on life – fuelling perfectionism, people pleasing, and the constant feeling that we are never enough, or always need to prove our self-worth. So how can you break the cycle? I looked into the question when I woke up to the fact that my own limiting expectations had led to an unremitting level of unhappiness, that seemed to permeate my whole life. So I'm going to share some of the powerful tools I discovered and developed in the process of getting myself out of the dark place I was in. I'm doing this to help you begin to change any unrealistic expectations that are getting in the way of your ability to be happy.

Firstly, I want you to take a moment to consider some of the expectations you have of yourself that are unrealistic.

Then take some quiet time to really look closely at your life, and ask yourself these questions:

- Are these expectations my own or someone else's?
- What areas in your life do you desire to be more successful in?
- Where could you step up and into your courageous self?
- What would you have to do, or who would you have to become to realise your dreams?

- What's really holding you back – your thoughts, old beliefs or resistance to change?

Go all in and tap into your heart's energy. You can click on the QR code at the end of this chapter, and find the meditation that has been designed specifically to help you relax and reconnect with yourself.

So many of us settle for situations or people that make us unhappy simply because we have a misconception that we have to live up to someone else's expectations, like settling for a loveless relationship when it makes you unhappy. You have a right to expect a passionate, intimate, fulfilling relationship, and then do whatever is necessary to create and maintain that.

As far as the work you do goes, you don't have to settle with your position if you know you are capable of handling more responsibility. You also don't have to settle for a situation where the effort you are putting in and the results you are achieving aren't being acknowledged. It's time for you to expect yourself to excel in ways that will get you noticed and promoted, then turn up with the energy that is going to get you seen as the impressive person you are.

The other thing you don't have to accept is your current level of health when you know you can feel more energetic and happy within your body. This starts with expecting yourself to eat a healthy diet and to exercise several times a week, and doing whatever you need to in order to get a good night's sleep. These are pretty basic things I know, but at the same time, they are critical components that contribute to the health of your body and your ability to live a life you'll enjoy.

When you start to take responsibility for your own emotional well-being, the universe will rise up to support you and you'll begin to open yourself up to a whole new world of opportunity and clarity. And I am not talking about something that is completely 'woo woo' here. It is actually a scientifically proven fact called 'Positive Synchronicity' that's at play when things just seem to fall into place. The idea of Positive Synchronicity was originally raised by Carl Jung, and then explored further by the Australian psychologist, Chris Mackey. He wrote that "When we have an expectation that something will work out for us, our inner world and the outer world become more synchronized than we might previously have thought possible, which then brings together a powerful energy that supports a positive outcome."

Honestly, you can tap into this, and believe me – It will change your life.

Setting Clear Shared Expectations:

What I'm going to share with you now is something Brene Brown calls 'Painting Done'. I call it 'Setting Clear, Shared Expectations'. Either way, it means to fully walk through our expectations of what the completed task, job, idea or dream will look like. The expectations need to include when it will be done by, and what will be done with the finished 'Painting'. This includes clearly communicating our expectations with others and, importantly, being open to listening to others. It's about sharing everything you can think of to paint a combined picture of the expectations that are required to fulfil the dream/idea you are working toward. Setting shared expectations relies on one of the most powerful tools we have – communication.

I know that engaging in this kind of communication can feel vulnerable, however making a habit of doing it will build courage and trust in yourself and others. And in their case, it will build a higher level of trust in you. It's a double whammy really. I say that because having the courage to practice the 'Painting Done' exercise will not only leave you with the result you were working toward, but also build meaningful connections with others. This is so important, because having a partner, friend, or colleague who truly has your back and with whom you can reality-check in with, is a priceless outcome.

The other side of the coin is that when someone expresses their dreams and hopes with us, what we are witnessing is true courage and vulnerability at the same time. So when we've shared an expectation with someone and we feel they have let us down, we mustn't close ourselves down. We need to keep the lines of communication open and talk about our feelings, and then move to the question of accountability by saying something like, *I tried to express how important this was to me however……….* It's important to stay open here and really listen to what they say when they respond. It's all too easy to become defensive and start communicating from a space of blame or shame.

Try to remember that communication is a tricky thing, because it could be that the 'filter' the person we're talking to is hearing what we say through, is giving them a totally different message to the one we think we have sent them. So be calm, and kind, and realise that everyone is only doing the best they can with the resources they have, ourselves included.

Meanwhile, if the shoe was on the other foot and it was your response to something someone said that's being flagged, then it's a great opportunity for you to ask for more information if you need it, and make sure that you practice taking responsibility for your behaviour, and simply apologise when an apology is required.

Sometimes the most uncomfortable learning is the most powerful.

Discovering honest expectations – both of yourself and others – is a transformative step toward greater self awareness and fulfilment. When you take the time to reflect on what you truly expect from your life, relationships, and work, you will uncover the hidden motivations driving your actions. Realigning these expectations with your intrinsic values will allow you to live with more clarity and purpose. In the next chapter, we will be unearthing your intrinsic values, so you'll be building on what we're covering here.

For now though, I hope you are beginning to understand how powerful expectations are.. They shape how we show up in the world and how we interact with those around us. Moving forward with a commitment to setting clear, realistic, and supportive expectations for yourself will foster a higher level of confidence and self-respect. Likewise, understanding and communicating your expectations with others will build stronger, more authentic connections.

Ultimately, your expectations are a reflection of what you believe is possible. When you choose to set empowering expectations, you will create the foundations for a life aligned with your deepest truths.

The bottom line is that you'll start to notice the synchronicity that unfolds when you set clear, honest, and supportive expectations – both within yourself and in your interactions with the world around you. Opportunities and connections will begin to align and show up in your life. Remember, what we focus on expands. So, I'd encourage you to keep exploring, refining, and holding space for the ever-evolving version of yourself that you are continuously growing into, and look for the incredible synchronicities that are going to show up for you.

REFLECTIONS

Here are four thought-provoking questions that will help you reflect on your expectations of yourself, your life, your business, or your career:

Are the expectations I set for myself realistic and aligned with my values, or am I striving to meet standards imposed by others or society?

_____

_____

_____

How do my current expectations support or hinder my growth, happiness, and sense of fulfilment?

_____

_____

_____

_____

_____

What would change if I allowed space for flexibility, compassion, and progress instead of perfection in my goals and daily actions?

_____

_____

_____

_____

_____

Where am I beginning to see the synchronicity in my life as I set realistic expectations and change my mindset?

_____

_____

_____

_____

_____

*Discovering your heart's true values
is not about becoming someone new;
it's about remembering who
you've always been.*

Chris Ross

STEP 6

CHAPTER 7

VALUES
Your Inner Compass

Looking back at some of the darkest moments after Tom's accident, I realised that I had unconsciously leaned on my intrinsic values to carry me through. One value that showed up repeatedly was my love of humour. I can't even count how many times a good laugh saved me from spiralling into my own destructive patterns. It's important to have something like humour to keep us afloat because grief is a silent and unpredictable fiend, creeping up unexpectedly and disempowering us if we let it. In my case it was laughter that was my shield – it was my lifeline.

One vivid memory still brings a smile to my face to this day. It was at Shenton Park, and Tom was in this old wheelchair, pushing it to its limits, navigating a tight corner at top speed on our way to physio. He lost his balance and began to wobble, nearly to the point of tipping over. My first instinct was panic. I rushed to save him, and in my frantic state, we both ended up in a tangled heap. But instead of the tears that were on the verge of spilling over, we just looked at each other and burst into fits of laughter.

In that moment, laughing was so much more supportive than crying could ever be. I've got to hand it to Tom, because even in his most vulnerable moments, he drew on his courage, and somehow, he still found a way to make his mum laugh.

We were also lifted up by the 'collective alignment of values' we share with our friends and family. Our sense of belonging, and the safety and warmth of being surrounded by people who truly cared was a lifeline for us. Without that kind of connection, without that network of love and support, my family and I would surely have drowned in our own despair.

Have you ever found yourself in a moment when all hope seemed to be lost, only to look around and realise that you were being held up by a connection-based values group? That sense of collective support is something that is so powerful that it can completely turn the tide when we need it the most.

In this chapter, we'll explore the various aspects of discovering your values, and how you can bring them together to unearth the intrinsic values that define you.

Unearthing Our True Values

Values are emotional states we strive to experience consistently. They serve as a compass, guiding us toward our truth and authentic identity. Our values are not something we acquire; they are innate, waiting to be uncovered. From the moment we are born, the mission to discover and align ourselves with these values is placed within our hearts.

When we are aligned with our values, we feel emotionally strong, clear, and connected. However, when we stray from them, emotional instability can arise, leaving us unprepared to face life's challenges, and just not feeling 'right'. Have you ever experienced this? Perhaps you've felt strong and clear in a decision you have made. This means the decision is aligned with your heart's values. Similarly, when you have felt a tingle of unease, or a sense that something is off, your inner voice is telling you that your intrinsic values have been rubbed up the wrong way.

Take a moment to consider this. We've all experienced this sense of something being a bit off in one form or another. We might call it intuition, or a deep knowing. We can choose to ignore it, or to trust our innate self when it comes to making the day-to-day decisions that shape the way our life turns out.

Over the past six chapters, we've made significant progress together:

You've envisioned the future your heart desires through conscious visualisation.

You unearthed the beliefs that both hold you back and propel you forward.

You discovered the inherent attributes within you that support and encourage growth.

You examined your standards – for yourself and others.

And finally, you reflected on your expectations, and considered whether they were realistic and empowering, or set so high that they sap you of your essence?

To really gain the highest result for this journey to discover your truth you've entered into by reading this book, I encourage you to really take the time to unearth your values using the meditation and the Reflection pages at the end of this chapter. This is about uncovering your values, not anyone else's – not your family's or your community's, but your own intrinsic values that reflect what really matters to you.

Knowing our values means we are clear on what matters and what doesn't. We become clear on our boundaries, and this leads us to having a deeper sense of certainty. Certainty is one of the most attractive qualities any of us can have. We listen to the one who is most certain – right? And in this case, that person is you!

When we are aligned with our values, we feel emotionally fit.

Here's the thing, we all find the time, the money, the energy and the space to have and experience what truly matters to us. We need no motivation to be, do and have what we want to experience in our lives. The question for most people is "Do you know what you truly want?" For most of us the answer is no, or I'm not sure.

Personal values represent what you hold to be important. Intrinsic values however, reflect the truth of who you are. They require courage because living by your intrinsic values means being loyal to your heart and your driving purpose. These values help you prioritise the demands of life and serve as a guiding light, influencing both your decisions and behaviour.

Many of us struggle to articulate the values guiding us – not because they don't exist, but because they're so deeply ingrained in our beliefs and worldviews that they often remain invisible. Becoming aware of the values that are driving your decisions in life is the first step to living in alignment with what truly matters to you.

As you uncover your values, you'll begin to let go of what doesn't serve you. You'll gain the courage to be the person you've always dreamed of being. You'll be able to communicate your desires and needs clearly, and you'll attract people and opportunities that align with your values. Whether it's in relationships, your career, or personal growth, values are the key to clarity, confidence, and fulfilment.

There are three types of values we all carry within us:

1. **Contribution-based values:** These are reflected in how you contribute to your community, family, or friends, through patience, kindness, creativity, or service.

2. **Connection-based values:** These lead to your sense of belonging, connection, and relationship with your family, career, or nature.

3. **Vitality-based values:** These are the things that energise you – fun, health, sports, or creative expression.

A balance of all three types of values is crucial to emotional well-being. To attract the right people, career opportunities, and abundance into your life, you must first align the way you are behaving with your values.

One key to achieving alignment is to ensure that your standards and expectations remain flexible. When we become rigid in our beliefs, standards, or expectations, it creates internal conflict leading to emotional instability. For example, if wealth and prosperity are your top priorities, but you neglect other areas of your life in pursuit of them, frustration, disappointment and fear may arise. True emotional well-being comes from balance and flexibility.

Think of a palm tree in a cyclone. Does it stand rigid, refusing to bend? No, it's designed to sway with the wind, allowing it to withstand the forces that could otherwise bring it down. In the same way, being flexible with our values and open to considering others' thoughts and perspectives, allows us to bend when necessary while staying rooted in what truly matters to us. This is what it means to be aligned with our true heart's values.

This chapter is the culmination of all the work you have already done in the previous chapters.

If you can set aside 15 minutes of undisturbed time for yourself, you will gain a deeper understanding of this final part of the journey, and you will change your life in ways you never thought possible. That's a big statement I know. But it's one I can attest to because of the results that have been achieved by myself and my clients. So, I implore you to finish this final part of the journey to truly understand what really matters to you, and why.

These are Your Values – not anyone else's, but your intrinsic values!

By now, you've gathered a wealth of insights about your beliefs, attributes, standards, and expectations. It's time to bring that all together and determine the values that resonate most deeply within you. They are the ones that will guide you as you move forward in life. Doing the work to dig down deep to uncover your values is about laying the foundation for taking control of your life. It will allow you to live by choice, and not chance. Values are the things that will inspire motivation, not manipulation. They drive change, not excuses. They help you choose self-esteem over self-pity.

Everything we've explored over the past five chapters comes together now. So let's begin the final step, where you'll elicit your core values – your inner compass to guide you through life using the Values Template in the Reflection Section.

REFLECTION

Take a moment to write your top 8 values in the left-hand column in no particular order. If you need some help, you can use the Values List you'll find at the end of this Reflection section to help you articulate your feelings.

Once you've listed them, go down the list and assign a number to each value, ranking them from 1 to 10, with 10 being the most important. For example, if someone believes family is a top priority, they might give it an 8 on a scale of 1 to 10.

It's okay if two or more values feel equally important at this stage.

Take your time with this exercise.

After you've ranked all your values, move to the third column.

This is where you'll get to see your values in their order of importance, starting with the highest-ranked value. It's not uncommon to have to grapple with the fact that several values could get the same score. If that's the case for you, I'd like you to sit with each one and feel into it. Let your heart guide you. For instance, if Health and Courage both scored a 10, take a moment to feel into which one resonates more deeply for you as the top value.

Once you have completed this exercise, take a moment to review what you've arrived at – are your values resonating with you? Has there been an 'ah-ha' moment?

Now for the fun part which is crafting your 'Power Statements'.

For each value, write a powerful phrase or sentence that captures its meaning for you. This statement will serve as

VALUES

your personal compass, helping you stay grounded when life's challenges or opportunities arise. You can use this exercise to see if they align with your values. It's a simple yet powerful way to articulate your intrinsic values and give them life.

Your values will become your guiding light, your inner compass guiding you through life's decision-making moments. Use these values in every aspect of your life and you will always be aligned with what truly matters to you.

YOUR VALUES IN ANY ORDER	RATE 1-10	PLACE VALUES IN ORDER OF PRIORITY	POWER STATEMENT

YOUR VALUES

This list is intended as a prompt for you. It's not exhaustive by any means, and if you feel your value is missing from the list, please add it. The idea here is to help prompt you to articulate something that feels aligned if you are struggling to name a value in your life. Have some fun with this.

Accountability	Courage	Heritage	Order
Achievement	Creativity	Home	Parenting
Activism	Curiosity	Honesty	Patience
Adaptability	Dignity	Hope	Patriotism
Adventure	Diversity	Humility	Peace
Altruism	Efficiency	Humour	Perseverance
Ambition	Environment	Inclusion	Personal fulfilment
Authenticity	Equality	Independence	Power
Balance	Ethics	Initiative	Pride
Beauty	Excellence	Integrity	Recognition
Being the best	Fairness	Intuition	Reliability
Being a good sport	Faith	Job security	Resourcefulness
Belonging	Family	Joy	Respect
Career	Financial stability	Justice	Responsibility
Caring	Forgiveness	Kindness	Risk-taking
Co-creation	Freedom	Knowledge	Security
Collaboration	Friendship	Leadership	Self-discipline
Commitment	Fun	Learning	Self-expression
Community	Future generations	Legacy	Self-respect
Compassion	Generosity	Leisure	Serenity
Competence	Giving back	Love	Service
Confidence	Grace	Loyalty	Simplicity
Connection	Gratitude	Making a difference	Spirituality
Contentment	Growth	Nature	Stewardship
Contribution	Harmony	Openness	
Cooperation	Health	Optimism	

Once you choose hope,
anything is possible.

CHRISTOPHER REEVE

CHAPTER 8

HOPE

Finding the Glimmer in Life's Darkest Moments

Hope is a word we often throw around, sometimes without realising the depth of meaning it holds. We speak of hope in everyday conversations – I hope this meeting goes well, I hope it doesn't rain, I hope I get the job. But when life hits us with unimaginable challenges, hope takes on a whole new meaning.

There was a time in my life when hope felt like a distant, unreachable thing. After the accident when our son Tom was fighting for his life and everything we knew seemed to crumble, I found myself lost in a sea of despair. The future I had imagined for our family was suddenly gone, and I couldn't see a way forward. Everything felt dark, uncertain, and overwhelming.

But here's the thing about hope. It doesn't always show up as a blazing light. Sometimes, it's a tiny flicker, just enough to guide you through the darkness. That's exactly what I learned.

Hope isn't about expecting everything to suddenly be okay. It's about believing that even in the most painful and uncertain times, there is a way forward. It's about trusting that despite the hardships, there is still beauty to be found, still moments of joy, and still a future worth moving toward – even if it looks different from the one you imagined.

The Flicker of Hope

There is one moment that stands out in my memory, a moment when I realised that hope was still alive, even if it was faint. It was after months of grappling with the reality of Tom's accident. I was sitting alone, reflecting on everything we had been through. I had felt so lost for so long, as though I was just going through the motions of life. But then I thought about Tom – his strength, his resilience, and how despite everything, he was still here.

The tiny spark of gratitude I felt about Tom having the ware withal to get through the accident that changed his life forever, ignited something within me. It wasn't a sudden wave of relief or joy, but it was a quiet reminder that there was still something to hold on to. That's the thing about hope. It doesn't erase the pain, but it offers a lifeline. It gives us the strength to keep going even when we don't know what the future holds.

Leaning Into the Light

As I reflected on my journey while writing this book, I realised that hope was never completely gone; it was simply hidden beneath layers of fear, grief, and uncertainty. And once I started to lean into the idea that hope was still there, even in the smallest moments of gratitude or laughter, I began to feel lighter. Not because the challenges disappeared, but because I no longer felt completely overwhelmed by them.

Hope is an anchor. It holds us steady when the storms of life threaten to pull us under. It doesn't deny the storm, but it gives us something to cling to as we navigate our way through it.

I know that you, too, would have faced moments when hope seemed out of reach. Maybe you're in one of those moments right now, feeling overwhelmed, and unsure of how to move forward. I want you to know that it's okay to feel that way. It's okay to sit in the uncertainty and the pain. But don't give up on hope.

Hope doesn't mean you have to see the whole path ahead. Sometimes, it's about trusting that the next step will appear when you're ready to take it. It's about believing that no matter how dark things may seem, there is light waiting to break through.

Nurturing Hope

So, how do we begin to nurture hope when it feels so far away? How do we keep that flicker alive when the weight of our struggles feels like too much to bear? The four points below are worth keeping up your sleeve:

1. **Shift Your Focus to Small Wins**: Sometimes, hope isn't about looking at the big picture. It's about noticing the small victories along the way – the moments of laughter, the acts of kindness, the simple joy of a quiet morning. These are the seeds of hope that remind us that life is still worth living, even in the midst of pain.

2. **Lean on Your Support System**: Hope often comes from connection. When I felt most hopeless, it was the people around me including my family, friends, and even strangers, who reminded me that I didn't have to carry the burden alone. So, reach out and let others remind you of the strength you've forgotten you have.

3. **Allow Yourself to Dream Again**: Hope is the bridge between the present and the future. When we allow ourselves to dream of a better tomorrow, we create space for hope to grow. Even if that future looks different from what we originally envisioned, it can still be filled with purpose, joy, and meaning.

4. **Start With the End in Mind**: By thinking about a positive outcome, you'll create a spark of imagination in your limbic brain that will ignite a little bit of hope to begin to grow. Really activating this process can result in life starting to open up for you in ways you never thought possible. This is the Positive Power of Synchronicity.

Hope as a Practice

Hope is not a passive emotion – it's a practice. It's something we must cultivate, especially in the challenging times. It's waking up each day and deciding to believe that things can get better. It's choosing to focus on what's possible, instead of being paralysed by what feels impossible.

And here's what I've learned. Hope isn't always loud. It doesn't always come with grand gestures or miraculous outcomes. Sometimes, hope is quiet. It's found in the small moments of connection, in the tiny steps forward, and in the decision to keep showing up, even when it's hard.

CONCLUSION
You Are Never Alone

I may not know exactly what led you to pick up this book, but I'm so glad you did. My deepest hope is that as you've read through these pages, you've felt even the smallest glimmer of hope begin to return. Whether you're facing a health challenge, the loss of a loved one, a career shift, or simply navigating an uncertain season of life, I want you to know this—hope is always within reach.

And you don't have to figure it all out alone. I understand what it's like to feel stuck in a place you never expected to be, to wrestle with questions that seem to have no answers. But I also know this: even in the darkest times, hope has the power to transform your path forward. Sometimes, life nudges us in a new direction, and other times, it pushes us so hard that everything familiar falls away. But no matter how it happens, we always have a parachute—even if we don't see it at first.

That's why I encourage you to scan the QR code below. When you scan it, you'll be taken to the **Book Bonus page**, where you'll find incredible resources to support you on your own journey. You'll also have the opportunity to connect directly with me through my booking page, where you can schedule a complimentary strategy session. This is your chance to gain clarity, rediscover hope, and take real steps toward the life you truly want to live.

You are not alone beautiful one. Let's take the next step together.

From my heart to YOU,

Chris Ross

ABOUT CHRIS ROSS

Chris Ross is a coach, speaker, and author passionate about helping others unearth hope and resilience in the face of life's challenges. Married to Peter, her quiet and steadfast support for over 37 years, Chris has navigated the highs and lows of life while raising two beautiful children, running three successful businesses, being an awesome grandmother, and weathering the unexpected that comes with it all.

Life hasn't always been graceful, in fact often messy, sometimes overwhelming—but always she's tried to approach it with deep respect, love, and a commitment to growth.

Through her own journey, Chris discovered that even in the darkest moments, hope is never out of reach. Her experiences, especially in the wake of her son Tom's life-changing accident, led her to rediscover what really matters in this life and that is Love.

Just an ordinary woman finding her own extra-ordinary.